INTRODUCING

Sociology

Richard Osborne • Borin Van Loon

Edited by Richard Appignanesi

Icon Books UK ◆ Totem Books USA

This edition published in the UK
in 2004 by Icon Books Ltd.,
The Old Dairy, Brook Road,
Thriplow, Cambridge SG8 7RG
email: info@iconbooks.co.uk
www.introducingbooks.com

Sold in the UK, Europe, South Africa
and Asia by Faber and Faber Ltd.,
3 Queen Square, London WC1N 3AU
or their agents

Distributed in the UK, Europe, South
Africa and Asia by TBS Ltd., TBS
Distribution Centre, Colchester Road,
Frating Green, Colchester CO7 7DW

This edition published in Australia
in 2004 by Allen & Unwin Pty. Ltd.,
PO Box 8500, 83 Alexander Street,
Crows Nest, NSW 2065

Previously published in the UK
and Australia in 1996 as
Sociology for Beginners and in
1999 as *Introducing Sociology*

Reprinted 1997, 1998, 2000,
2002, 2007

This edition published in the USA
in 2005 by Totem Books
Inquiries to Icon Books Ltd.,
The Old Dairy, Brook Road,
Thriplow, Cambridge
SG8 7RG, UK

Distributed to the trade in the USA by
National Book Network Inc.,
4501 Forbes Boulevard, Suite 200,
Lanham, Maryland 20706

Distributed in Canada by
Penguin Books Canada,
90 Eglinton Avenue East, Suite 700,
Toronto, Ontario M4P 2YE

ISBN-10: 1-84046-583-2
ISBN-13: 978-1840465-83-9

Originating editor: Richard Appignanesi

Printed by Gutenberg Press, Malta

What is Sociology?

Beginning sociology is rather like learning to ride a bike. Once you've done it, it seems easy, but incredibly difficult to explain to someone else. Or growing up, which seems natural, just like riding a bike, but incredibly difficult to explain to someone who doesn't know.

What sociologists attempt to do is explain the different forces and influences that shape how someone grows up.

In other words, sociology is about explaining what seems obvious – like how our society works – to people who think it is simple, but who don't understand just how complicated it really is.

Imagining Sociology

How do you *do* sociology? First you need a good sociological imagination. You have to think of human society rather than of personal experience. Think hard and imagine yourself as a Siberian coal-miner working in minus 20c temperatures and not being paid for six months.

What would be yo
reaction to this and to th
break-up of the o
Communist Sovi
Union

If you can imagine what it is like to live on boiled potatoes and cabbage for six months, not be paid and not even be able to watch MTV, then you've probably got a sociological imagination.

You will also need some idea about how people function in groups, and some idea about how to do research.

The ability to look at society like an alien would help as well.

Was Communism a good thing or not? This is an important question that needs some imagination, some history and some sociological theory. It is an interesting sociological question because Communism was an attempt to rebuild society completely – which is what sociology is rather interested in.

Before sociology was invented as a means of thinking about society, everyone more or less accepted society as it was.

The debate about how much one can reshape society is rather central to the sociological project.

The problem of sociology is understanding why society functions at all, and why people accept society's control.

What is Society?

Communism, capitalism, the free-market, the mixed economy are all different forms of society that we often discuss. But the key question is: "What is society?" In fact, where is it? The former Prime Minister of Britain, Mrs Thatcher, famously doubted the very existence of society.

There is no such thing as society. There are individual men and women and there are families.
February 1989

On the face of it, she seems right. If you look around, all you immediately see is people doing things by themselves. But if you look harder, you see **groups of people** acting in very organized ways.

If you believed individuals could do whatever they liked, you would ultimately have to approve of any sort of bizarre behaviour, including murder.

Most people, including Mrs Thatcher, actually believe that the way society is organized is terribly important. This is why individualism is something of an illusion.

Individuals exist, but they are socially made. This is the basic conundrum of sociology. Commonsense attempts to span this divide, but never very successfully. The family is always taken as the "building-brick" of society.

> The family is a natural thing and it's just commonsense to support it.

> But what is commonsense?

> You start with some obvious ideas, and an explanation of why people believe them, and end up with a complex theory of how people think.

Once you start to question the way that human beings interact, and the way they behave, then you find yourself in a theoretical mess. Human culture is very, very strange once you stand outside commonsense and consider what people actually do. That is exactly what sociology asks you to do.

So what is missing from commonsense? A theory of how people work and live together is missing. Why don't people just kill each other, for example? Why do some people conform strongly to dominant cultures and other people reject them totally? There are clearly different societies with different cultures, and so we need a theory that explains the difference between societies and people's reactions to them. In a nutshell, that is what sociology is.

Why Am I Unemployed?

Persons who become unemployed often feel at fault, that *they* have failed in some way. They think of the problem in an individual way. This is a commonsense view, but there are many complicated reasons why somebody might be made redundant.

Reasons to do with social change at the wider level, rather than any individual problem.

In a Communist society, an individual explanation for unemployment would be less accepted than in a capitalist society where the commonsense view is that the individual is wholly responsible.

Sociology would set out to analyze the individual and social patterns that produce unemployment.

Surplus Labour

The reasons for unemployment could be ...

1) Technological change (new machines)
2) Changed work practices (efficiency)
3) Work done in other countries (globalization)
4) Political change (government policy)
5) Cultural change (different products wanted)
6) Lack of requisite skills (no access to education/retraining)

None of these has anything to do with the individual worker.

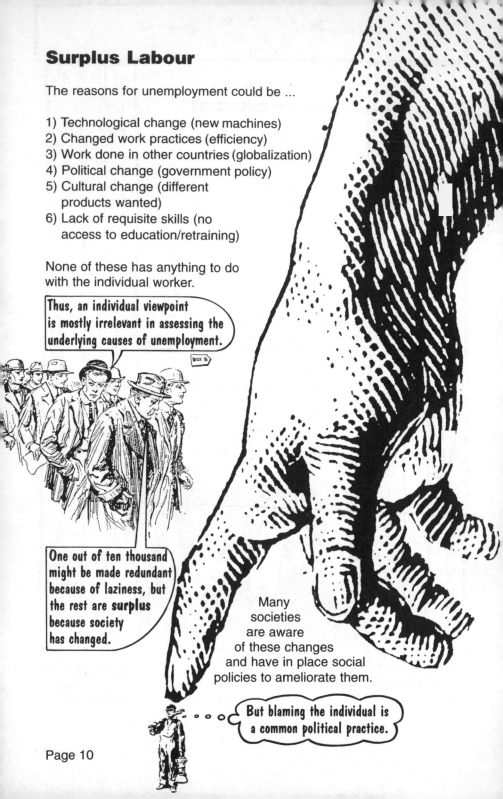

Thus, an individual viewpoint is mostly irrelevant in assessing the underlying causes of unemployment.

BOX B

One out of ten thousand might be made redundant because of laziness, but the rest are **surplus** because society has changed.

Many societies are aware of these changes and have in place social policies to ameliorate them.

But blaming the individual is a common political practice.

Industrial Change

We are all aware that the societies we now live in are changing rapidly and that the world our parents knew has probably disappeared for good. What causes these changes and how we react to them is a central theme of sociology. The discipline of sociology grew out of a realization that societies **do change**, beginning in the modern era with the French and American Revolutions.

In the 18th and 19th centuries, America and Europe changed from being agricultural societies into industrial ones.

This was a very major shift, the consequences of which we are still living through.

Sociology is an overview way of asking, "What caused that to happen?" and "Why do people do things like that?"

The Problem of Ideology

Sociology has got a bad reputation, and many people, particularly politicians, claim that sociology just states the obvious in a complicated way, using a lot of theory.

This may sometimes be true, but more often than not it is politicians who avoid trying to understand things ...

My friends, I stand for blind prejudice and commonsense ideology.

Sociology threatens ordinary understanding of how things work, and that is why it irritates many people.

This problem of commonsense and the inability to link individual problems to wider sociological structures is what we call the problem of "ideology".

False Consciousness

The word "ideology" has many meanings but they all tend to describe how people believe certain things about the world that may well not be true. Commonsense ideas about the world are frequently ideological, in the sense that they are belief rather than scientific description.

The belief that black people are less intelligent and genetically different to white people is an ideology. It is not a scientifically justified set of ideas.

Many of the views people hold about society, and how things should work, like marriage or schooling, are based on ideologies rather than abstract thought about culture and social behaviour.

KARL MARX

I describe ideology as **false consciousness**, by which I mean people believe things that are untrue and which delude them about their real social position.

Workers believed that the upper classes had a right to exploit them and that this was just the "way of the world". Sociology is really a **critical awareness** of social life.

Comparing Differences

Once you accept that social behaviour isn't innate, or natural, or just commonsense, then you have to start thinking about how we might understand different societies. Wherever you start with social behaviour, you find that the way people behave is influenced by previously existing ideas and cultural patterns.

We learn our social behaviour in the family. The phrase "bringing up children" actually means teaching them how to behave like proper social beings.

Once you compare different groups – like social classes or societies in Britain and India – you soon realize that there are many different ways of "bringing up children". Comparing and analyzing different ways of doing things is an important sociological approach.

How to Approach the Study of Sociology

It is often said that sociology is the **scientific** study of society and human behaviour, but it is not really clear what that means. The first question is, how do you study society?

What is society? I've been looking for it everywhere and nobody wants to talk to me.

You can't study society. You can only study people and how they interact.

Ah, I know what you mean. Society is just an abstraction, you can't see it.

Society is structure and power. You can see it in action. The police are a symbol of society's laws and methods of control.

The Law and Society

As an example, take a look at judges. They have been around in different forms for a very long time. When they are locking people up, judges often say ...

You are a danger to society!

or ...

Society must be protected from people like you.

Now if Mrs Thatcher were right and society didn't exist, then people obviously shouldn't be locked up for being a danger to it.

Either the judges or Mrs Thatcher have got it completely wrong.

The law is an important part of society that governs how things run or are supposed to run. So sociology wants to say, "How do these things work? Why do judges make the decisions they do? How do prisons work and why do people commit crimes? Is it because they are bad, hungry, or because they saw it on television?"

Sociology's Judgement on Judges

The legal system is an institutionalized form of behaviour with deep historical roots. Societies are basically made up of clusters of institutionalized forms of behaviour, which are reproduced and changed in time.

What sociology would see in this clash between the law and a member of an ethnic minority are issues of culture, of ideology, of social control and of social action.

The Origins of Sociology

The things that sociologists say have always been discussed by philosophers, poets, novelists and even religious leaders. Plato prescribed how society should be organized 2,500 years ago.

Modernity

To put it crudely, we can say that sociology is the reflection of "modern" societies. By this we mean that only when society had been transformed into a recognizably "modern" or "industrial" society was it possible to begin to reflect on how that transformation had happened.

Modernity and industrialization undermined the old settled order of agriculture and religion and began to speed up all of the technological and cultural changes that had developed over several centuries.

We can say that modernization (and the tricky new bit, "postmodernity") is simply that process of change constantly speeding up.

Sociology is the descriptive science of urban societies.

To put it another way, sociology wasn't invented by cavemen (or women) because they didn't have the intellectual tools to do it. It was during the intellectual revolution we call the "Enlightenment" that change, progress and critical thought all combined to lead people to the realization that society, like everything else, was "man-made" and therefore changeable. In criticizing the old order, a new vision of society was born, and the French Revolution gave a real stamp of approval to these radical new approaches.

The guillotine put into practice the radical ideas that some people had about social re-structuring.

You are about to be re-structured. It won't hurt a bit!

Who Founded Sociology?

So what are sociology's methods? Who are its founders? What led to the rise of sociology? The English, French and American Revolutions set off the questioning that eventually led to the birth of sociology.

It is not surprising that the French were the founders of sociology, since their social revolution in 1789 was the most radical and shocking of them all.

We can trace the origins of sociology back, amongst others, to **Baron Montesquieu**'s work *The Spirit of the Laws* (1748), in which he considered the "nature and principle" that underlay different kinds of laws, and therefore, societies.

My radical proposal was to consider the different institutions in society and how they influenced each other or interacted.

From this idea, it wasn't a great intellectual distance to think about society as a whole.

David Hume, Empiricist philosopher (1711–76)

Most thinking about social forms had just concentrated on specific areas, like the economic or the religious. To begin thinking "encyclopaedically" was in itself revolutionary!

As everybody knows, it was really the Scottish Enlightenment that started it all!

It's all a question of, is sociology a science, and what does that mean, or is it just interpretation and analysis that may be able to tell us about the future?

It is a pseudo-science which just describes obvious social change using lots of long words and a few statistics.

It is a grand theory that tries to explain everything about human development through analysis, comparison and theoretical evaluation of social institutions.

It is a male-dominated profession that seeks to explain social development in terms of male categories, like work, wealth, war and industry. It is completely blind to women and their work, and their social roles.

Where do we start?

Positivist Sociology

The philosopher **Auguste Comte** (1798-1857) is recognized as having coined the term "sociology" itself. He grew up in the years following the French Revolution and was clearly influenced by the radicalism and turmoil of the time, as well as reacting against it.

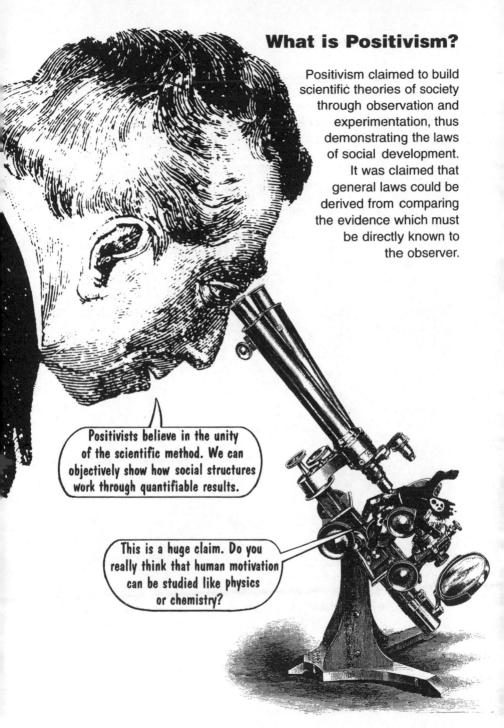

What is Positivism?

Positivism claimed to build scientific theories of society through observation and experimentation, thus demonstrating the laws of social development. It was claimed that general laws could be derived from comparing the evidence which must be directly known to the observer.

Positivists believe in the unity of the scientific method. We can objectively show how social structures work through quantifiable results.

This is a huge claim. Do you really think that human motivation can be studied like physics or chemistry?

The Organic Model

Comte strongly believed that a scientific approach to understanding society would lead to orderly progress. He also insisted that society should be seen as a system of interrelated parts. This was based on his idea that all societies could be seen as developing in an evolutionary manner from a **theological** stage, through a **metaphysical** phase, to a positive or **scientific** stage.

This evolutionary outlook assumes that societies, like organisms, develop from the simple to the complex.

This organic analogy sounds quite plausible, but is now generally considered to be just another 19th century fantasy.

Comte was right about one thing though – that sociology is the most general, and the most difficult, of all human sciences.

Comte, and Spencer after him, believed that one had to look at "consensus" in society, or the total integration of the system as a whole.

Page 26

Comte actually used the term "sociology" in the fourth volume of his *Cours de Philosophie Positive* (1838). He was certain that sociology was a new science and he would be hailed as its founder. He was half right on both counts. The argument about whether sociology is a science or not still rages, although most are now pretty certain that it isn't.

A Preview of Feminist Criticism

Anticipating the much later feminist critique of sociology's masculine bias and approach, **Harriet Martineau** (1802–76) published a work that had little impact at the time but became recognized as an interesting comparative analysis of social structure.

It was an early instance of what we might now call cultural studies, an important branch of sociology.

Evolutionary Sociology

Herbert Spencer (1820–1903) was the next big name in the sociological Hall of Fame, but somebody who went out of fashion almost as quickly as he came in. The reason for both was that he advocated evolutionary theory to explain social development.

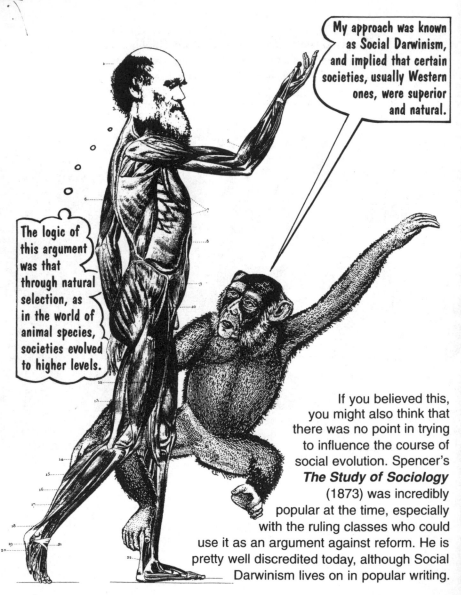

My approach was known as **Social Darwinism,** and implied that certain societies, usually Western ones, were superior and natural.

The logic of this argument was that through natural selection, as in the world of animal species, societies evolved to higher levels.

If you believed this, you might also think that there was no point in trying to influence the course of social evolution. Spencer's *The Study of Sociology* (1873) was incredibly popular at the time, especially with the ruling classes who could use it as an argument against reform. He is pretty well discredited today, although Social Darwinism lives on in popular writing.

The idea that society is "natural" or like an organism is terribly strong, both in commonsense views of the world and in the sociological theories that today we call **socio-biology**. Spencer, like Comte, was impressed with the natural sciences. Biological metaphors about society seemed to go hand in hand with scientific procedures.

What starts out as a respect for science, which seems fine, ends in the theoretical and political disasters of eugenics, racism, and ultimately, the holocaust.

Socio-biology, in all of its different forms, is simply the re-emergence of crude ideas about "survival of the fittest" and of genetically superior races. We are now certain that all of humanity shares common ancestors and DNA, which makes these eugenicists and their socio-biology seem just a little unscientific.

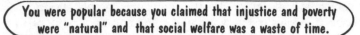

You were popular because you claimed that injustice and poverty were "natural" and that social welfare was a waste of time.

Exactly, and my ideas keep coming back, like Thatcherism and Reaganism, and books like **The Bell-Curve** and all those debates about how some races have a lower IQ than others.

BELL CURVE (JUST IN CASE YOU DIDN'T GET THE ALLUSION)

You argued that society should be seen as a system, which is right, but the rest is Victorian social Imperialism, and proof of how pseudo-science can be a powerful ideology in social formations.

Spencer's grand theories have had little influence in sociology, except perhaps in **functionalism** (examining the social "function" of an institution within society). Sociology's search for general laws of society, and its sense of itself as a unified and all-encompassing science, are what make it very unpopular with historians, economists, philosophers, psychologists and politicians.

It is odd that despite claiming to be scientific, sociologists have rarely spelt out the kinds of laws and generalizations they claim to aspire to.

Physics has got many general and provable laws; sociology has a few generalizations and a lot of grand claims.

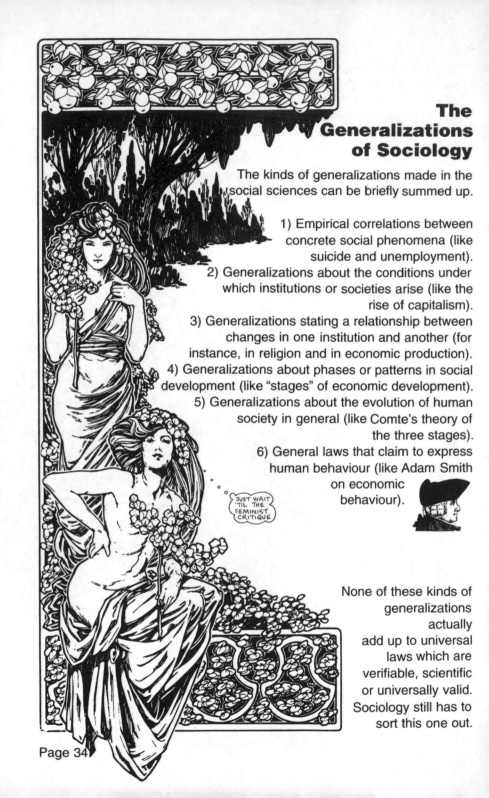

The Generalizations of Sociology

The kinds of generalizations made in the social sciences can be briefly summed up.

1) Empirical correlations between concrete social phenomena (like suicide and unemployment).

2) Generalizations about the conditions under which institutions or societies arise (like the rise of capitalism).

3) Generalizations stating a relationship between changes in one institution and another (for instance, in religion and in economic production).

4) Generalizations about phases or patterns in social development (like "stages" of economic development).

5) Generalizations about the evolution of human society in general (like Comte's theory of the three stages).

6) General laws that claim to express human behaviour (like Adam Smith on economic behaviour).

JUST WAIT TIL THE FEMINIST CRITIQUE

None of these kinds of generalizations actually add up to universal laws which are verifiable, scientific or universally valid. Sociology still has to sort this one out.

The Contribution of Durkheim

One important sociologist who attempted to establish scientific laws in a thorough way, and to professionalize the subject, was **Emile Durkheim** (1859–1917). He was a follower of Comte in seeking scientific certainty. He also became the first Professor of Sociology at the University of Paris – or anywhere. He too was concerned with "consensus" and seeing society as a system.

Durkheim on Suicide

Durkheim's best-known work on suicide will give us a picture of what he was aiming at.

I decided to take this seemingly very individual act of ending one's life to see if there were any social patterns or forces at work. What are the moral pressures at work on the individual?

Could I just ask you a few questions? A little survey ... it won't take long.

I'm just a bloody statistic to you, aaaahhhh.

We positivists need our daily statistics.

In his famous work *Suicide* (1897), Durkheim looked beyond the individual act to the social factors that underpinned it. By comparing statistics from different societies, Durkheim showed that there are regularities in the patterns of suicide which demand attention.

Notably, Catholic societies had a lower rate of suicide than Protestant — the explanation being the strength of community and the anti-individualism of Catholicism.

Durkheim was here seeking to draw out the empirical correlations he had established between social integration and the suicide rate.

Whether he did so or not is still debated. Some argue that what Durkheim demonstrated was that certain societies represent things in different ways.

Not beef again ...

CORNY

Altruistic Suicide

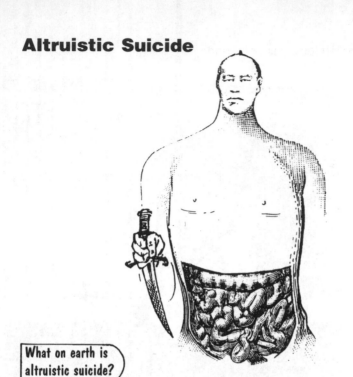

What on earth is altruistic suicide?

This takes place in a society where the social bonds are very strong, what I call "mechanical solidarity". This is suicide done for the sake of the group, rather like the Japanese ritual suicide, *seppuku*, when things have gone wrong.

Anomic and Egotistic Suicides

Social Facts

Durkheim was very keen to demonstrate the workings of what he called "social facts", which he described as "ways of acting, thinking, and feeling, external to the individual, and endowed with a power of coercion, by reason of which they control him".

This means that certain structures in society are so powerful that they control the actions of individuals and can be studied objectively, as in the natural sciences.

This was positivism at its most extreme.

ARMCHAIR SOCIOLOGIST

Whether there are any social facts in Durkheim's sense is still a matter of debate.

You positivists never get past the observable facts to understanding or explanation.

But you can't deny that I demonstrated a direct correlation between forms of society and suicide rates.

You leave out entirely what the individual thinks.

Society has a force of its own — individualism is an illusion.

Mechanical and Organic

Durkheim adopted an essentially collectivist approach to understanding society which involved different forms of "solidarity". Solidarity operates in various societies like a "social

In primitive societies, there is a form of "mechanical solidarity" at work. Society functions as a relatively close-knit affair.

Solidarity

glue" – the values, customs and beliefs that everyone in a society shares in a collective binding. This is also the **collective conscience** or group outlook which holds the individual in place.

As society becomes more complex, through the **division of labour**, mechanical solidarity breaks down and is replaced by organic solidarity.

In more complex industrial societies, social cohesion was clearly going to be a bigger problem. Economic interdependence in modern societies produces social cohesion but is also open to debate.

Structural Sociology

As an established "founding father" of sociology, it was right and proper that Durkheim should found a sociology journal (*L'Année Sociologique*) and write a very great deal on many subjects. His first book was *The Division of Labour in Society* (1893), dealing, somewhat strangely, with the moral basis of changes in the division of labour. Right through to his *The Elementary Forms of the Religious Life* (1912), Durkheim is always concerned with the collective function of any social activity, with the social facts and the moral unity of things.

Durkheim represents the **structural** pole of the "structural" versus "social action" debate that runs throughout all of sociology. The other pole argues that it is only from **individual action** and motivation that society is formed. This debate can also be represented as the "consensus" versus "conflict" debate, in which society is either seen as an integrated whole composed of structures which fit together in a comprehensible way, or as basically structured around conflict.

Individuals or groups are seen as battling to define society in their own interest, which means that society is not necessarily stable or integrated.

Marx's view of class conflict sees society as basically made up of opposing forces which constantly struggle against one another until strikes, revolutions or wars break out.

Marxian Sociology

The "conflict" approach to sociology was developed in the 19th century by **Karl Marx** (1818–83). He wrote a very great deal about economics, capitalism, culture, technology, class struggle and ideology. He also greatly extended that part of sociology which was concerned with grand theory, the evolution of humanity, and the possibility of reconstructing society in an entirely different mode.

I also claimed that my approach – **historical materialism** – was a truly scientific methodology which put me alongside Comte and Durkheim as a grand theorist.

We can accuse Marx of ultimately producing the most totalitarian societies of this century, despite setting out the most radical rhetoric of all time. Mind you, he was mega-correct about how technology would change the world!

Marx was primarily interested in social development and social change, and believed that wealth and power were unequally distributed in society. He was therefore not interested in how social consensus functioned but in how one group in society maintained its dominance over another. In some ways, he had a functionalist approach in that he saw certain institutions in society as functioning to maintain cohesion.

But a cohesion that gives control to a specific group — the ruling classes!

It was Marx who most strongly argued that people's commonsense views of the world were coloured by the ideology or viewpoint of the dominant groups in society, and that this produced false consciousness.

Social Renewal

We can briefly sum up Marx's sociological approach.

1) All societies are founded on conflict.
2) The basic motor of all social change is economic.
3) Society should be seen as a totality in which the economic is the determining factor.
4) Historical change and development is not random, but can be discerned in man's relationship to economic organization.
5) The individual is shaped by society, but can also change society through rational action based on scientific, historical materialist premises.
6) Work in a capitalist society produces alienation.
7) By standing outside society, through critique, human beings can understand and alter their historical position.
8) Therefore, through scientific critique and revolutionary action, society can be rebuilt.

This idea of **social renewal** has proved to be a powerful idea in the 20th century.

Capitalism: a World-Wide System

Marx's central proposition was that capitalism was a new form of social organization based on exploitation of the workers by the owners of capital. The capitalist bourgeois class extracted surplus value from the workers, the proletarian class, and aggressively expanded and developed the technologies of production, thus creating a **world-wide system**. This is a very different picture of society to that painted by Durkheim or Comte.

MONEY TALKS, EH?

My central argument is that the ways in which humans organize their economic production determines the overall shape of the society.

This is known as economic determinism.

What Marx meant was that the forms of economic organization – capitalist production for example – determined the law, politics, culture, religion and ideology of society. This is a sociological claim of a strong universal law, which many other sociologists disagree with.

The Profit Motive

Marx's sociology of capitalism argued that the profit-making production of commodities led inexorably to an entire social system that was a reflection of this pursuit of profit.

> Now that the water we drink is owned by capitalist enterprises who make huge profits from selling water (which generally falls out of the sky), you can see what Marx was getting at.

> Newspapers, television and radio, which were once thought of as providing information, or even being a public service, are totally geared to profit-making.

The values of capitalist production penetrate all spheres of society and set the agenda for the way that things are done. Retirement homes for old people are now big business, and making money determines how many staff and what level of care is on offer. This is what Marx means by the economic **infrastructure** determining the **superstructure** – or culture, politics, law, ideology, etc.

Class Relations

Marx brought into sociology the very important idea of **class**, as opposed to groups, strata, élites or caste. Marx asserted that the membership of a social class was determined by the **division of labour** in a society. Capitalism instituted a particular, and Marx argued, particularly exploitative, set of class relations. He argued that class was ...

1) An objective, external criterion.
2) Determined by relationship to the **means of production**.

3) Also a subjective criterion.

All owners of capital share the same relationship to non-owners — that of **exploitation**.

Class is a category that can exist but not be perceived by the members of that class. Bourgeois ideology obscures the reality.

A Theory of Totality

For Marx, capitalist society inevitably produces **class antagonism**, rather than consensus, and because of the very structure of that society, conflict and disharmony are inevitable.

Marx synthesized everything that economists, political theorists and philosophers had to say about society to produce a grand sociological theory of capitalist society as a totality.

His arguments pervade much of sociology because he touched, directly or indirectly, on every area of thought within sociology's domain.

Marxist ideas on ideology, knowledge, culture and power still provide much of the framework within which sociological debates go on.

Important 20th century figures like Gramsci, Adorno, Althusser and Habermas carried on this Marxist framework of thinking.

Weber's Sociology

Max Weber (1864–1920) was also very concerned with stratification in society, but he took issue with Marx's views on society and class struggle. Unlike Marx, he wasn't terribly politically active and didn't claim to have solved all of the problems of how society functioned. His first work, ***The Protestant Ethic and the Spirit of Capitalism*** (1906), distinctly parted company with Marx about the origins and development of capitalism.

I argued that it was the rise of a particular religious outlook, namely Protestantism, that distinguished certain societies and led them to develop capitalism.

The Protestant ethic had an **affinity** with capitalism, Weber argued. Marx instead argued that religious ideas were the **product** of certain economic conditions.

Religion is the opium of the masses!

On the contrary, religion can be progressive and lead to social change. Protestantism was one such religion.

Understanding Social Action

Weber redefined the theoretical approaches of sociology and did specific work on class and stratification, law, religion, capitalism, power as it is exercised in society, the city, music and cross-cultural studies. Unlike Marx, who probably never used the word sociology, Weber systematically set out a philosophy of the social sciences and attempted a complete definition of sociology. He was interested in the way people behaved, and in how their behaviour influenced the wider society, as well as in social structure.

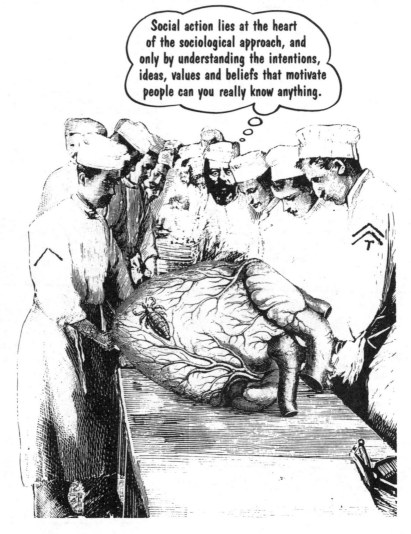

"Verstehen"

Suppose a poor, badly educated and "alienated" child throws a brick through Weber's window. "Why did you do that?", Weber asks him.

Weber's concern with "understanding" (the *Verstehen* concept) may seem straightforward, but it leads to that sociological approach we now call the "social action" approach – a complicated sense of how cultures and individuals interact.

Bureaucracy

The other very important area in sociology that Weber pioneered was the study of the way in which modern societies become bureaucratic or controlling – the "Big Brother" syndrome. This also related to Weber's other big concern with **rationalization**.

Why was that important?

Just get a ticket, stand in line, fill out the application form giving three references and we'll consider your application to ask a question.

I'm not really that interested.

In that case, fill out the withdrawal form, stand in line and fill in the application form to be considered for withdrawal.

Rationalization

Capitalist societies become increasingly like an "iron cage". **Rationalization** is the process by which every little part of society is subjected to analysis, organization, professionalization and bureaucracy.

Just as Marx used to point out that the rationalized reorganization of production led to alienation, so Weber was concerned at the way in which the state constantly intervened more and more in the life of its citizens. Fritz Lang's film *Metropolis*, Charlie Chaplin's *Modern Times* and Terry Gilliam's *Brazil* all deal with this topic in different ways.

The Spectres of Communism and Bureaucracy

Despite his attacks on Marx, Weber often sounds like him when he is talking about rationalization. It has a determinist ring to it. This is odd, because Weber claimed to be mainly interested in understanding social actors' motives, not socially determining structures. Weber often seems to argue that culture is more determinant than the economic in shaping society. But culture sometimes seems to include the economic as an important shaping factor. Certainly Weber's arguments, like Marx's, can be seen as a product of the times he lived in.

Germany in this period, 1870–1918, was going through major changes and industrialization, and the rise of a large Communist party.

Weber's attitude to Marxism may well have been coloured by his fear of a Communist revolution, but also of the rise of a bureaucratic state in which individualism would be squashed.

If we are polite, we can say that he could see both sides of the argument — and perhaps an extra one as well!

Weber was also very concerned with political groups, the complexities of social status and the "charisma" of leaders – an idea of uncanny prescience, given the rise of Hitler.

My attitude to sociology as a discipline can be summed up like this ...

1) It could not develop scientific laws (anti-positivism).
2) It could not predict or evaluate future social development.
3) It could only use collective concepts like "class" if they could be discussed in terms of individual action.
4) It could not prove any evolutionary development in human societies (anti-organicism).
5) It should construct models or "ideal types" that could be compared.
6) It should aim for objectivity by systematic empirical research (by being "value-free").
7) It could not draw on the natural sciences because society was about "consciousness", not "structures".

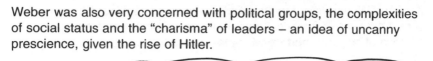

Marx and Weber differ fundamentally. Marx was convinced that there were "iron laws" of historical and social development and therefore a "science of society", **historical materialism**. Weber contradicted him on every point.

Sociology is a science concerning itself with the interpretative understanding of social action, and thereby with an explanation of its causes and consequences.

So all sociology is about social action, about the ways and means in which people interrelate within different kinds of societies.

Trying to understand the different ways in which people relate within society leads inevitably to trying to **classify** different kinds of society.

Tönnies: Social Classification

Another important German sociologist was **Ferdinand Tönnies** (1855–1936), whose interest in the forms and patterns of social ties and organizations resulted in classifications of particular societies. Societies were either *Gemeinschaft* (community) or *Gesellschaft* (association).

A *Gemeinschaft* society is one in which social relationships are close, personal and valued by their members. The family is the basis of social networks, with social conformity as the norm. This sort of community is typical of pre-industrial society. The Amish in America today are representative of this form of society.

BOOK!! BOOK!!

YOU'RE MY BESHT MATE, YOU ARE...

A *Gesellschaft* society is instead one in which close family associations have disappeared and in which social relationships tend to be impersonal and non-kinship based. Social ties arise from an elaborate division of labour in which the work-place is more important than the extended family.

Tönnies' basic theme is the **loss of community** and the **rise of impersonality**. This became very important in the study of the city.

Changes in Sociology

We might add "post-industrial" society to Tönnies' classification system, but we are not altogether sure how social relationships will work (if they do) in this newly emergent form of society. Analyzing the kinds of social relationships in a particular society is one way of classifying what sort of social system it is. Throughout the history of sociology, theorists have tried to classify different societies into neat systems. Comte began it with an idea of development towards the perfectly rational society. Marx encouraged it by saying you defined a society by its "mode of production" or form of economic organization. Durkheim distinguished between "mechanical" and "organic" solidarity. Weber said you could classify different types of authority as "traditional", "charismatic" and "bureaucratic".

The question is, is it possible to classify a whole complex society by one set of characteristics?

In simple societies, definitely; in later societies, probably.

CHANGES IN SOCIOLOGY

Can you see the coming chaos — the mass emigration to America?

When sociology emigrated to the United States in the 20th century, it found new problems and new methods. 19th century European sociologists had been preoccupied by societies in which large, powerful social groups or classes predominated with entrenched interests and cultures. American society was fundamentally more fluid and socially open. This is why 20th century social development and theory has always tended to look towards the American model for inspiration, rightly or wrongly. European society had taken millennia to develop. American society evolved overnight and without all that much awareness of where it was going. 19th century theorists could never have imagined the whirlwind of development that America initiated, in which traditional society was replaced by a mythology of the "frontier".

Native American culture took thousands of years to develop and little more than 100 years to destroy.

That is the other side of modernization.

The Spread of Mass Industrialization

Since Marx and Comte were writing at the beginnings of mass industrialization, it is not entirely surprising that their sociological views quickly dated. Marx's belief in inevitable revolution did not stand the test of time. Weber was quite certain that there was no inevitable process of revolutionary change.

I can be seen as the sociologist who straddles the emergent societies of the 19th century and the increasingly complex and contradictory societies of the 20th.

Changes in the post-war era have made many of Weber's concerns seem antiquated as well, but the central debates about the individual and society, rationalization and alienation, determinism and action, religion and ideology, still reverberate throughout sociology. Debates about the work of the founders still go on, but everybody in sociology admits that it moves and changes with the social context. In other words, sociology has always to reinvent itself.

Sociology became popular in the United States largely because it was a society of high-speed change, development and experimentation. It was also a pragmatic, capitalist society that worshipped production and economic expansion. In one sense, American society had to be invented, since it had no history or organic development, but in another it was firmly based in European models. Perhaps because of its lack of roots, sociology in America concentrated on empirical study, trying to capture the factual details of what was really happening rather than building grand theories of human development.

Individualism and individual struggle were also greatly emphasized in American culture and philosophy.

It is a bit of a mystery, then, that Functionalism, which so much assumes social order and cohesion, should have become the mainstream theoretical approach in America.

The Technological Revolution

The unleashing of technology, which Marx had correctly identified as the dynamo of development in capitalism, reached its fruition in the United States, and in so doing produced a new and radically different society. Henry Ford's production lines, and the new rationalized time-and-motion studies in the steel industries, were the harbingers of social change so radical that sociologists were forever trying to catch up.

It is not an exaggeration to say that virtually every aspect of modern capitalist society has been restructured and transformed almost every decade since the 1930s.

The pace of change has also accelerated each decade so that in the 1990s, three-year-old technology is redundant!

Compare this with some agricultural technologies that have been used for 2,000 years in the Third World and you get a picture of the sociologist's task.

Teaching sociology is like giving a lecture on flying to the passengers on a jet that is crashing.

Social change, social reform and social surveys are at the basis of all sociology, and all three were clearly evident in the industrializing and urbanizing America of the late 19th and early 20th centuries. One could also see the Protestant ethic at work in the cultural legacy of the early Puritan fathers of the East Coast. This ethic of hard work, thrift, sobriety and avoiding the sins of the flesh was, as Weber had argued, consistent with the spirit of capitalism. 20th century America absorbed millions of migrants, massive expansion and a history of slavery and exploitation. This explosive mix was somehow made to work, for better or worse.

Sociology is a barometer of how people feel about society. It veers between orthodoxy and conservatism, with very occasional flashes of radicalism.

Pioneers of American Sociology

An odd character called **Lester F. Ward** (1841–1913) played an important role in the early history of American sociology. His whole career was spent working for the United States Geological Survey.

I set out to identify the basic laws of social life, drawing on Spencer's approach, but I was also an advocate of social reform.

Two other Americans of early major influence were **W.E.B. Dubois** (1868–1963) and **Jane Addams** (1860–1935). Both conducted detailed empirical surveys which clearly demonstrated what people's living conditions were actually like. The function of this investigative research – actually demonstrating what was happening in society – should not be underestimated.

Especially because many people either don't want to know or like to believe something else.

This is particularly true where racist discrimination is concerned.

For a long time, polite sociologists didn't talk about the history of slavery and colonialism.

W.E.B. Dubois' study *The Philadelphia Negro* (1899) carefully depicted the actual living and working conditions of black people, the reality of racism and discrimination.

I was the first black sociologist to gain academic acceptance and was also active in the National Association for the Advancement of Colored People (NAACP).

Jane Addams' famous *Hull House Maps and Papers* (1895) were a detailed documentary of the slum conditions in Chicago's West Side.

My survey gave impetus to social reform.

Her work was similar to **Friedrich Engels'** classic *The Condition of the Working Class in Britain* (1844).

Research that demonstrates what is actually happening in society becomes more important all the time, because as society gets ever more complex, individuals know less and less about how other people really live. The mass media seem to cover everything, but it is debatable whether they increase or decrease knowledge about actual social conditions. The American insistence on empirical investigation was highly productive in many senses, but constantly ran up against commonsense ideas and entrenched ideological positions.

It was recognized that social reform was necessary, however, and this gave added impetus to the growth of sociology as a discipline in the United States.

Sociology is always directly affected by the political climate of the times, unlike biology or physics.

The Chicago School

The first department of sociology in America was founded at the University of Chicago in 1892. It was famous for two things: its urban studies – not surprising given its place in a large city – and its championing of **symbolic interactionism**, which was a little surprising. Urban studies could take Chicago itself as a "laboratory". This same interest led to a concern with symbolic interactionism, which describes the way in which people interact in a face-to-face situation.

When you live in a crowded city you obviously have more interaction than if you live in the middle of nowhere.

Urban Sociologists

The Chicago sociologists did not look at society as a whole, or a mega-system that controlled everything, but at smaller groups and how they made sense of their place in society. Because Chicago was a rapidly growing and multi-ethnic society, they could see before their own eyes a whole new social process. Immigrant cultures set up their own sub-groups in ghettos where standard white American ideas were out of place. The Chicago school produced a series of studies looking at groups and gangs seen as deviant or non-conforming.

To do this, we had to engage in direct study and develop a new theoretical approach that took account of the way in which people defined their new situation.

People develop and define their group identity through **interaction** — a mutual working out of what things mean.

This is the creation of the "social self".

This is what **symbolic interactionism** is all about.

Culture and Meanings

The meanings people give to their cultural and social activities are as real in their consequences as economic forces and natural forces. Wage rates may seem very real, but then so are people's ideas about what work is and what leisure is. Religion is the most extreme example of the power of ideas, for which people have died throughout history.

Chicago school analysis is very concerned to look at how individuals' perceptions of their situation shape their culture and group responses.

We see people as self-conscious cultural actors.

So if people believed that the only way to survive in a new society was to band together and flout society's rules, then that could be seen as a form of rational response.

The Mafia is the most extreme form of this kind of group culture.

It's hard to remember how radical the Chicago school seemed at the time, and not just as "moral relativists".

Urban Studies

Understanding how a city functions became increasingly important in 20th century sociology, for obvious reasons. The Chicago school, and especially **Robert Park** (1864–1944), came to dominate urban studies. Park developed what he called the "ecological approach", by which he meant that the city somehow adapted itself in an orderly fashion, like ecological processes in the environment.

The city is, it seems, a great sorting and shifting mechanism, which, in ways that are not wholly understood, infallibly selects out of the population as a whole the individuals best suited to live in a particular region and a particular milieu.

Louis Wirth (1897–1952), another Chicago school sociologist, viewed Urbanism as "a way of life", similar to Weber's "impersonal" city life. This idea, prevalent in modern sociology, that the city stands for alienated, impersonal social relations, is something of a myth. Cities vary as much as the so-called countryside and change as rapidly as any other part of society. The underlying assumption that all city life is fast, dangerous and unpleasant, whilst all country life is slow, charming and friendly, does not stand up even to the most elementary empirical research. Inner city life can be friendly, cosmopolitan, interesting and socially interactive, as opposed to isolated, alienated, hard country life.

Symbolic Interactionism

The Chicago school's interest in **symbolic interactionism** had precisely to do with the sorts of meanings that individuals give to their environment. In other words, the question of identity and socialization – or how people **learn** their culture and reproduce it. While much of 19th century sociology concerned itself with the "grand schemes of things", symbolic interactionism saw itself as bringing things down to the basics – to individuals and how they make sense of the world.

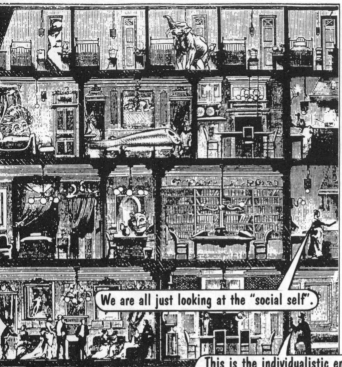

We are all just looking at the "social self".

This is the individualistic end of social theory, which sees society as constructed of the individual's acts and intentions.

It fits in with American ideas of the free spirit and an open society.

The "Social Self"

George Herbert Mead (1863–1931), the man responsible for this approach, pointed out that man is the only species that can use **language** and therefore plan, think and communicate about experience.

As we develop as individuals, we learn to use the symbols of our immediate group and to give them the same meaning.

As we and society develop, these symbols and their meanings can change. Thus we **symbolically interact** with our environment.

Mead came to look at society in a way similar to that of Freud and psychoanalysis, but with a behaviourist twist. How the personality developed was seen as the central building-block of all social theory. Mead patented a theory of the self as constructed and reconstructed through interactive behaviour.

Childhood shapes the personality forever.

The self is always in process.

Am I Self-Made?

Mr Mead, tell us about your theory.

It's about understanding the development of the self, the person, and imagining yourself in other social roles.

By having a sort of internal conversation with yourself — about "significant" other people and other roles — you develop an idea of how everything works. Children do it very easily because they like to play roles and pretend to be other people. This is practising for growing up.

Exactly. The development of the self is a process between the "I" and the "Me".

So it's about human agency — how I shape "Me" in relation to others.

A SELF-MADE MAN WORSHIPPING HIS MAKER?

All this stuff is fine, but it completely ignores the real pressures that society puts on people. You can't just **choose** to be a certain kind of person. All previous sociology showed how people are a product of their situation. Your interactionist theory is only extreme individualism dressed up as group relations.

Not at all. You've missed the point.

The self can only develop in its interactions with other people, so that the self really is social — part of a group, a sub-culture, a wider culture. That's the point. Without other people to learn from, since the earliest days of childhood, there is no way for an individual to acquire a sense of self.

It's still all a bit voluntary though, isn't it? As though you can choose who you'll be today?

Not at all. Each socialized person ...

... is a society in miniature!

Symbolic Interactionism and Psychoanalysis

The symbolic interactionist approach, like psychoanalysis, is part of the attack on social system theory that happens every so often in sociological battles. The real difference is that psychoanalysis believes in the power of the Unconscious to shape the individual, whereas the interactionists see it as a more conscious process. Both approaches give due importance to the problem of **socialization**, or how children are trained to become proper people and citizens. Both suggest that the clue to understanding society lies in the mind and the individual's appropriation of external reality.

Psychoanalysis believes that childhood and the family define most of society's functioning.

Symbolic interactionism says that the personality isn't fixed, but fluid.

Psychoanalysis was pretty big in the States, but sociologists steered clear of all that sexuality stuff. They have a bad enough reputation as it is.

The Individual

There are two reasons for looking at socialization and how the personality is formed. One, it is the point that commonsense begins with; and two, we have to understand the individual before we can comprehend the social. **Pliny the Elder**, the Roman encyclopaedist of the 1st century A.D., long ago said the same thing.

Human individuals, unlike most animals, are totally dependent creatures for an extraordinarily long time. It is this fact that makes the process of socialization so important, by which the helpless infant acquires a cultural identity and becomes a self-aware, independent person.

Nature vs. Nurture

Do we just "naturally" do things, like learn language? There is very little evidence for that argument. There are a few recorded instances of children being brought up by animals and behaving like them. These stories demonstrate that becoming a civilized human being is **learnt**.

If learning is arrested in the early years, there is little chance of fully recovering from it.

The process of learning is a very long one involving parents, schools, the mass media, friends, college and peer groups.

Who has the most influence is an important debate in sociology. The question "how is a personality formed?" underlies what we call the "nature" versus "nurture" debate.

The nature supporters claim genetics and hormones make boys and girls. The nurture lobby say that it comes from social engineering.

How Does Socialization Function?

Socialization is a key concept in sociology. It connects one generation to another and hugely influences the developing shape of society.

In fact, it is the only way in which society and culture **can** be reproduced.

It is an area of constant moral panic over popular culture and other influences which supposedly shape a delinquent or deviant generation.

Traditionalists argue that discipline is necessary for children. Others argue that affection and tolerance are the way to produce rounded social selves. Sociology has to try to assess how socialization **does** function and what its long-term impact is on the personality.

Freud's Theory

For Freud, the developing relationship of the infant to the mother and father profoundly affects the psychological make-up of the child. This in turn affects later development through the power of the Unconscious. The main sociological point here is that the creation of the personality, even in its hidden parts, is fundamentally **social**.

Freud's idea is that the human personality is formed in a reciprocal relationship with the parents. In acquiring a sense of self, the infant picks up social ideas about gender and behaviour. To be human means to develop a "self" from relationships with others.

That infant sexuality is at the basis of all human development is clear to me.

Freud claimed to have discovered infant sexuality and the Oedipus Complex that goes with it. Not everybody agrees.

Much mainstream sociology dislikes Freud and psychoanalysis, probably because if Freud were right about the unconscious and its effects on the social, much of empirical sociology would be beside the point. Similarly, symbolic interactionism is not wildly popular because it undermines a lot of grand theories and sociological research projects. Actually, Mead didn't use the term symbolic interactionism – it was invented by one of his followers, **Herbert Blumer** (1900–87). He put forward three main propositions.

Human beings act towards things on the basis of the meanings that things have for them.

The meaning of things is derived from the social interaction that one has with one's fellows.

Group action takes the form of a fitting together of individual lines of action.

This approach and urban sociology fitted together because they were against formal surveys, statistics and controlled projects. Both preferred the individual approach.

Functionalism

Sociological approaches seem to produce their opposites in historical terms, and symbolic interactionism was counteracted by functionalism. This latter approach almost entirely ignored the individual and concentrated on society as a **system**.

From the earliest days of sociology, the functionalist perspective has been important, perhaps because it approximates to a commonsense view of the world. This means that functionalists believe that all social institutions have a **purpose** within society – like the family – and that understanding this function is what sociology is all about. Functionalists in America, like Talcott Parsons and Robert Merton, are mainly interested in the large-scale structures of society – social classes, economic institutions, governments, armies etc., and are not so interested in the individual. Their work is obviously influenced by Comte, Spencer and Durkheim, and can be called **social structural**.

Functionalism became the dominant ...

... theoretical approach in America during the 1940s and 50s, but in the 1960s interactionism, ethnography ...

SPARE CHANGE, GUV?

... and feminism began to undermine it.

Talcott Parsons

Talcott Parsons (1902–79) systematized earlier formulations of functionalist approaches to sociology, often in an obscure, dry and pseudo-scientific fashion. He started from the "Hobbesian problem of order", harking back to the philosopher **Thomas Hobbes** (1588–1679).

Hobbes thought people would naturally probably rip each other apart unless socially controlled and restrained. Parsons' major book *The Social System* (1951) set out at great length what he called the functional prerequisites of a society's survival. These were:

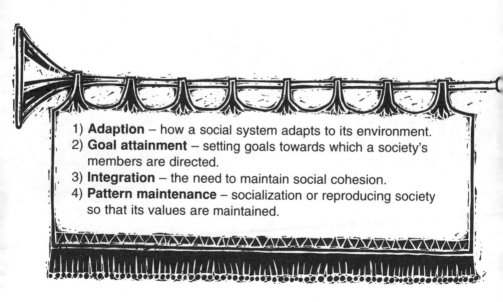

1) **Adaption** – how a social system adapts to its environment.
2) **Goal attainment** – setting goals towards which a society's members are directed.
3) **Integration** – the need to maintain social cohesion.
4) **Pattern maintenance** – socialization or reproducing society so that its values are maintained.

Equilibrium

In trying to answer the question about social change, Parsons produced ingenious explanations to show how things could change but stay the same. This was his theory of **equilibrium**. This theory suggests that changes in one part of the system produce counter-actions in other parts of the system which return it to equilibrium – even if it is a *changed* equilibrium.

Parsons also accepted social evolution, like Spencer and all the other 19th century evolutionists who thought we were evolving towards more complex, superior societies.

The case for a functionalist approach is that it does try to explain how society reproduces itself. New generations are born all the time that have to be socialized, educated, and taught how to become a part of society and how to find a role.

I harnessed Freud to discuss this problem of socialization.

Although this might seem radical, Parsons simply adapted Freud to back up his contention that the "function" of the family was to reproduce the young into a properly functioning society. His use of Freud certainly made psychoanalysis more acceptable to mainstream sociology, but his version made it seem as though the nuclear family were the only system available for child-rearing.

Parsons said that social life is characterized by "mutual advantage and peaceful cooperation", but he was completely wrong in his explanation.

Functionalism as an approach is the nearest thing that sociology ever had to a complete consensus, and Talcott Parsons was the king. During the golden years of the 1940s and 50s, everybody in America was a "functionalist", because everybody believed in the family, home-cooking and mother's place in the kitchen.

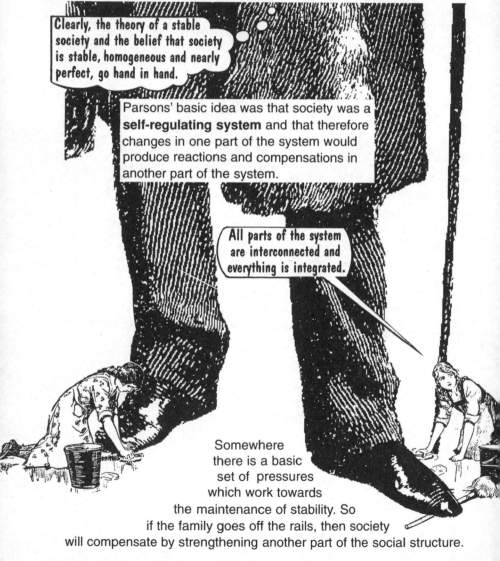

Clearly, the theory of a stable society and the belief that society is stable, homogeneous and nearly perfect, go hand in hand.

Parsons' basic idea was that society was a **self-regulating system** and that therefore changes in one part of the system would produce reactions and compensations in another part of the system.

All parts of the system are interconnected and everything is integrated.

Somewhere there is a basic set of pressures which work towards the maintenance of stability. So if the family goes off the rails, then society will compensate by strengthening another part of the social structure.

Functionalists like to make tidy arguments about everything and make lists of the functional prerequisites of society. These latter are the basic necessary conditions of existence which a society must meet if it is to survive, in the way that a plant needs air, water and soil in order to survive. These supposedly "universal" functional prerequisites of society are, of course, very like the hard facts and general laws that one finds in physics and which "hard" sociologists are always eager to invent.

If you believe that society and all its members must be seen as a total system, then the functionalist approach becomes essential, and understanding conformity is a functional prerequisite of being a sociologist.

Unfortunately, the 1960s blew a hole in this normative utopia because hardly anyone conformed to it.

CANNABIS SATIVA

HE'S A DOPE FIEND! WE'D BETTER KEEP AWAY FROM HIM!

The idea that you can only study any part of the system in relation to the whole is actually what Marxists say in a different way.

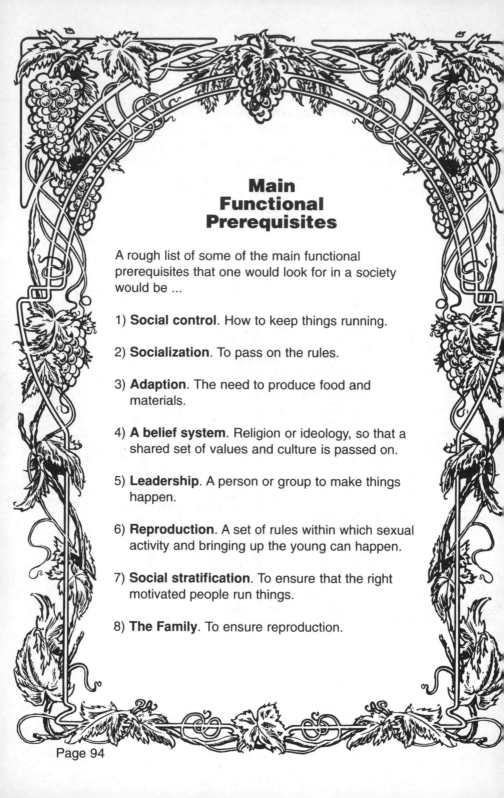

Main Functional Prerequisites

A rough list of some of the main functional prerequisites that one would look for in a society would be ...

1) **Social control**. How to keep things running.

2) **Socialization**. To pass on the rules.

3) **Adaption**. The need to produce food and materials.

4) **A belief system**. Religion or ideology, so that a shared set of values and culture is passed on.

5) **Leadership**. A person or group to make things happen.

6) **Reproduction**. A set of rules within which sexual activity and bringing up the young can happen.

7) **Social stratification**. To ensure that the right motivated people run things.

8) **The Family**. To ensure reproduction.

Merton's Functionalism

Robert K. Merton (b. 1910) was a functionalist who tried to answer two fundamental questions that ultimately undermined the whole enterprise. Why should we view society as a whole? And why should we assume a tendency towards conformity and integration? In trying to answer these questions, he put his finger on the basic fallacy of functionalism – the *myth of coherence.*

There were three main problems, which in the wordy way of functionalists Merton called "fallacious hypotheses".

1: **The postulate of indispensability** (you can't leave it out). This begs the question of how far any particular social institution actually reflects a "functional" or "essential" prerequisite of social order.

> This becomes a tautology, since in order to understand the function of something in society, you already assume it **does** have a function, which then explains why it's there. But if it weren't there, it wouldn't have a function.

> Functionalists try to have their structure and eat it.

> Or which comes first, the function or the function?

Merton's fallacy number 2: **The fallacy of functional unity**. In other words, why on earth should we assume that societies are integrated, coherent systems? Many societies are clearly nothing of the sort. How can functionalism explain societies that appear to be in constant conflict?

Or if the "manifest" explanation doesn't work, talk about the "latent" (or hidden) function to get you off the tautology hook. War may have a manifest function of attacking the other side, but its latent function might be to bring everyone together in the long term.

Fallacy number 3: Sometimes called **"the postulate of universal functionalism"**, or why does everything have to have a function? Does somebody collecting Barbie dolls have a function for the maintenance of society? Why isn't it just mindless, irrelevant stupidity?

What Merton says in response to the universal functionalism question is that one can distinguish between functions (or **eufunctions**) and **dysfunctions**. He argues that the functionalist approach isn't necessarily about how society actually works but is really just a method of analysis. You can distinguish certain areas of behaviour that could be dysfunctional in a society and yet not be a problem for the overall analysis.

So, how do you decide what is dysfunctional and what isn't? Claiming that deviance or criminality, for instance, actually has a **function** for society is weird. Yet, that's exactly what Durkheim said about crime.

Does Inequality Have a "Function"?

Functionalists also argued that inequality was found in all societies and was therefore necessary. Class, stratification, élites, whatever you want to call it, fulfilled a function which functionalists described as making sure that the best people were in the top jobs. This bit of tautologic nonsense greatly endeared functionalists to those who ran things.

Which brings us to the really serious charge against functionalism. Was it simply an acceptance and an apology for the status quo?

Functionalism was unhistorical, uncritical and unable to examine the real complexities of people and society.

The real question that functionalism never answered is why societies change so much and apparently so randomly.

Conflict Theory

Functionalism's inability to explain conflict, disharmony, power relations and class war meant that as a theoretical approach it had distinct limitations, as well as some strengths. Conflict Theory, in reaction to functionalism in the 1950s and 60s, pointed out that society was made up of conflicting groups who slugged it out most of the time, rather than functioning as one big happy family. The conflict theorists argued that the real focus of all social activity was conflict over land, resources, wealth, the means of production, water, housing, education, etc.

Marxian Conflict Theory

Marx was one of the original conflict theorists, made plain in the *Manifesto of the Communist Party* (1848):

> The history of all hitherto existing society is the history of class struggles.

Most modern sociologists think this is going a bit far, but agree that conflict rather than consensus is the basis of society.

Georg Simmel (1858–1918) is also an important figure here.

> We would argue that conflict has become institutionalized in modern society, and it is this process that gives some stability to the social order.

> Power, politics and social institutions are therefore seen as **dynamic** rather than **functional**.

> Society isn't a system or an organism, it's a battle, which the rich usually win.

A Value-Free Sociology?

A French mathematician called **Henri Poincaré** (1854–1912) described sociology as "the science with the most methods and the fewest results". This upsets sociologists who like to claim that they always base their work on empirical evidence. It is always the "other side" who engage in too much theoretical argument. Sociology is meant to be synoptic, but it hardly ever produces analyses that everyone (or anyone) agrees with.

This is very odd for what is meant to be a science.

That's because sociology's object of study — society — changes faster than sociology itself.

Sociology is inevitably forced to be a self-reflexive subject.

It is also true that however much sociologists like to pretend otherwise, they are implicated in what goes on in society. Something can only be value-free if it is conducted in a cave 5,000 miles from anywhere, and even then there are shadows to contend with.

Towards Postmodernism

There is in fact a "sociology of sociology" (or **sociology of knowledge**) which looks at the rise and fall of the different theoretical explanations that analyze society. Since the decline of functionalism, which was clearly linked to the conservatism of the post-war boom years, sociology has increasingly fragmented into numerous different approaches. Marxism, symbolic interactionism, feminism, ethnography, urban studies, neo-Marxism, structuralism, semiotics and postmodernism have all fed into the post-60s unravelling of a fixed discipline. As society changes ever more quickly, methods of understanding it obviously need to keep pace, yet often don't.

Jean Baudrillard (b. 1929) says we now live in a society which is completely hyperreal.

This means that traditional sociology gets nowhere, because no one even knows what really goes on in society now, never mind understanding the function of it!

C. Wright Mills

C. Wright Mills (1916–62) provided a critique of both the status quo in sociology and of the self-complacent power élites in America, and also an historical interpretation of the development of American sociology. His famous work *The Sociological Imagination* (1959) savaged the complacency of functionalism and its cosy relationship with power élites in an attack that set the tone for the revival of critical sociology in the 1960s. Social inequality and élites go hand in hand, and clearly a sociology that is deeply critical of wealth and power will not be popular with the state and political élites.

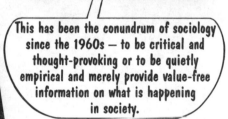

This has been the conundrum of sociology since the 1960s — to be critical and thought-provoking or to be quietly empirical and merely provide value-free information on what is happening in society.

If sociology is doing its job properly, then it should annoy those in power, since it exposes what is actually happening.

Post-1960s Developments

Before we disappear into Baudrillard's simulacrum, there are some salient points about the post-1960s development of sociology that need to be considered. Among the more important are the return of Marxism, the rise of feminism and the development of an anti-colonialist theory of historical development.

Sociology had long talked about industrial society, capitalism and modernization, but seemed to have forgotten that much of this was built on the back of an Imperialism that subjugated the Third World in order to pay for such development.

The slave trade stands out as an historical thread that connected Britain and America to their colonies without ever impinging on the advanced social consciousness of scientific sociologists.

Feminism likewise lobbed a large theoretical hand-grenade into the fountains of functionalism, and blew up slightly more than a Parson's nose!

Marxism underwent many extreme mutations during the 20th century. It was stifled by Stalin and mangled by Mao, but somehow came up smelling intellectually of roses during the 1960s. Many people put this down to the obscure charm of the anti-bourgeois intelligentsia, from **Antonio Gramsci** (1891–1937) to **Jean-Paul Sartre** (1905–80). But it may also be because of the stifling conformity of mainstream society and sociology. We do not need to remind readers of the parlous state of academic sociology which advocated things like "the end of class", "the end of ideology" and the near-perfect state of everything in society.

Marxism obviously came as a total relief to this suburban fantasy of conformity.

The other main point was that the sociological approaches derived from New Left Marxism were not connected to the politics of Communist countries, and produced critiques both of socialism and capitalism.

Marxism, despite its flaws, is essential to sociology, because sociology is centrally about industrial society.

The End of Ideology

Perhaps the high point – or the low point, depending on how you look at it – of sociology as conformity was what came to be known as the "end of ideology" debates of the late 1950s and 60s. **Daniel Bell** (b. 1919) in his book *The End of Ideology* (1960) put forward the idea that class ideologies naturally declined in capitalist societies and that a convergence towards power-sharing and social harmony took place.

> Better wages, the welfare state and general prosperity supposedly reduce alienation and bring about a higher stage of society.

> And new technology will lead the way towards a new utopia.

Just as these ideas were gaining ground, the wars, anti-authoritarian movements and social criticism that were to ignite the Western world during the 1960s began to unravel the political consensus. The convergence thesis now looks like wishful thinking, and in fact inaugurated an unprecedented period of conflict and rapid change in society and sociology. Sociology turned once again to Marxism, conflict theory and ideas that challenged the status quo.

Gramsci's Concept of Hegemony

Marx had originally argued that capitalist society would become ever more polarized between workers and bourgeoisie. Since this fairly clearly did not happen in the West during the 20th century, but rather the opposite, Marxists began to rethink how capitalist society functioned. It was increasingly recognized that society was becoming more, rather than less, complex and that there were more classes and intermediate groups in society.

Antonio Gramsci (1891–1937) was a key thinker in redefining the debate about class and power. His concept of **hegemony** has come to be central in sociological discussions of the complexity of modern society.

I pointed out that the bourgeoisie did not rule by **force alone** but also by **consent**, forming political alliances with other groups and working ideologically to dominate society.

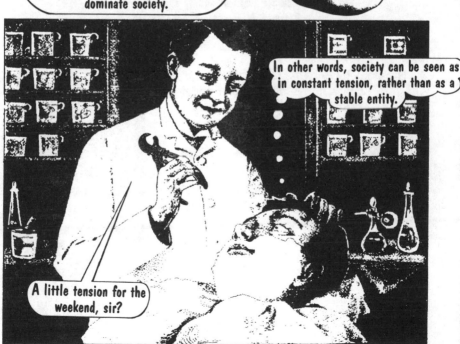

In other words, society can be seen as in constant tension, rather than as a stable entity.

A little tension for the weekend, sir?

Gramsci replaced Marx's notion of inevitable class struggle in society with a more flexible, rather sociological, view of the conflicts between groups, parties, individuals and ideologies. The idea of hegemony, or winning leadership by consent in society, draws attention to the fact that individuals are always reacting to and redefining the society and culture they live in.

ABSOLUTELY GRATUITOUS VISUAL METAPHOR COMPANY

Ideologies aren't simply injected into passive subjects who live them out — they are areas of debate and battle between dominant and subordinate groups in society.

His ideas have had a lot of influence in cultural studies and in discussions about popular culture — which is no longer considered just "circuses for the masses".

Gramsci wrote most of his theories in prison and had to disguise what he was saying. This makes interpretation just that little bit more difficult.

The Frankfurt School

This group of German critical theorists were mostly ignored when they wrote in the 1930s and 40s but began to be noticed in sociology in the 1960s. Like Gramsci, they were concerned with the problem that society, although capitalist, did not seem to be displaying the simplistic revolutionary development that Marx had predicted.

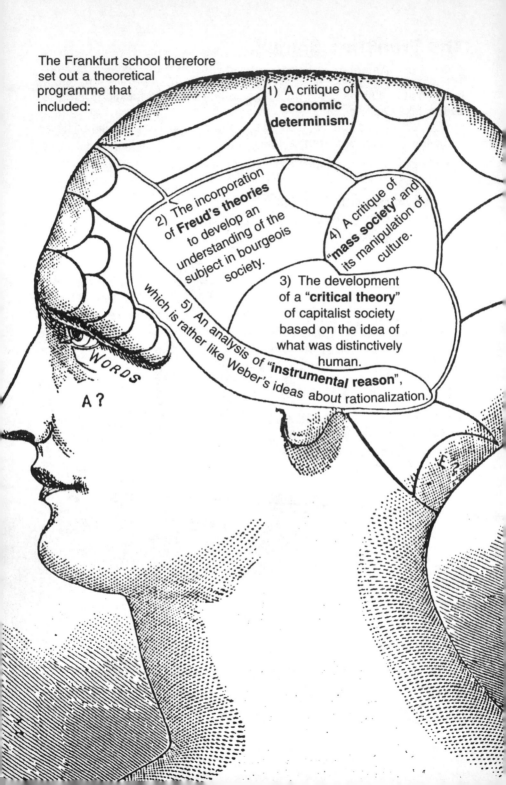

The Frankfurt school therefore set out a theoretical programme that included:

1) A critique of **economic determinism**.

2) The incorporation of **Freud's theories** to develop an understanding of the subject in bourgeois society.

4) A critique of **"mass society"** and its manipulation of culture.

3) The development of a **"critical theory"** of capitalist society based on the idea of what was distinctively human.

5) An analysis of **"instrumental reason"**, which is rather like Weber's ideas about rationalization.

WORDS

A ?

The Frankfurt school were also rather philosophical, and emphasized the importance of culture and ideology in shaping the individual in mass society, but many felt that they were too pessimistic in their gloomy view that mass culture was blinding everyone to the realities of life. The rise of Fascism and of what they called the "culture industries" seemed to them like similar signs of a new type of society that controlled its members through sophisticated cultural manipulation.

We argued that only "high culture" still retained a critical view of society, a sort of ivory tower against the debasement of the new media culture.

THE THING ABOUT WAGNER'S MUSIC IS THAT IT'S A LOT BETTER THAN IT SOUNDS...

Their central argument about modern culture and the mass media is clearly an important one in modern sociology, but perhaps Gramsci's ideas about **contested culture** are more appropriate. In terms of sociological theory, their inter-disciplinary approach somewhat messed up the neat approaches of empirical sociology.

Herbert Marcuse (1898–1979), a semi-detached member of the Frankfurt school, became very famous during the 1960s for his support of radical and anti-authoritarian causes. He was once called the "grandfather of terrorism", a reference to his critique of capitalist society, *One Dimensional Man* (1964), which brought together the arguments of the Frankfurt school that capitalism generated false needs, false consciousness and a mass culture that enslaved the working classes.

Unlike the others in the Frankfurt school, however, I argued for an authentic opposition and for liberation.

His *Eros and Civilization* (1955) is an important work in the debate about sexuality and society, and in *Negations* (1968) he attacked sociology's pretensions to understand society. He is really a bridge between the old theoretical concerns of European sociology and the re-worked radicalism of the 1960s.

Jürgen Habermas

Post-1960s sociology increasingly became aware of culture and communication as significant factors in analyzing society. **Jürgen Habermas** (b. 1929) combined these concerns with those of the Frankfurt school. He was concerned with **rational communication** and the possibilities of it existing in capitalist society. Unlike the older Frankfurt school members, he was not completely pessimistic about such a possibility. In his *The Theory of Communicative Action* (1981), Habermas puts forward a complex analysis of capitalist society and the possible means whereby the effects of instrumental reason (the rationality of Weber) can be resisted through moral and communicative emancipation.

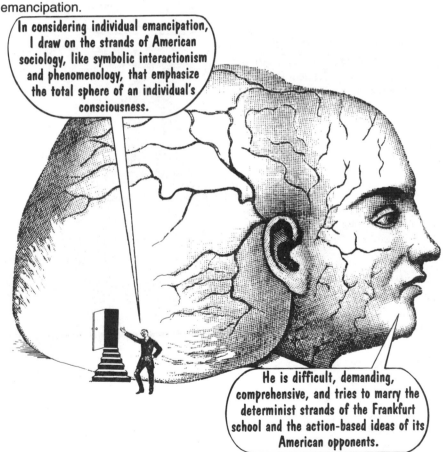

In considering individual emancipation, I draw on the strands of American sociology, like symbolic interactionism and phenomenology, that emphasize the total sphere of an individual's consciousness.

He is difficult, demanding, comprehensive, and tries to marry the determinist strands of the Frankfurt school and the action-based ideas of its American opponents.

The Structuralist Approach

After the neo-Marxist shift in sociology came the second wave of structuralist theory, which once again rewrote the ways in which social determination and social agency were conceived. The pioneering work in linguistics of **Ferdinand de Saussure** (1857–1913) began as a study of language but ended in studying almost everything as structure, including society. Saussure's theory of **semiotics**, or the study of signs, filtered into sociology in the post-1960s shift into pluralistic theoretical approaches.

> Seen as highly theoretical and "continental", these structuralist approaches have not been popular with some sociologists.

> But, particularly through the work of **Roland Barthes** (1915–80) and **Claude Lévi-Strauss** (b. 1908), structuralism has had a strong impact on many areas of sociology.

Starting from the famous axiom that language is a structured system, culture was then examined as a similar structured system, and then eventually society as a whole.

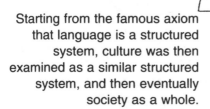

The most relevant part of the structuralist enterprise for sociology is in the area of cultural studies, or as sociologists say, in the analysis of culture as a signifying system. If this sounds baffling it may be because this kind of approach wants to "defamiliarize" the ordinary social world by looking at the way things "signify" or come to have a meaning within culture.

A word, "dog", signifies dogginess because our language system, through its rules and conventions, arbitrarily says it does.

Everything, like a "flower", has a meaning because of the language system within which we operate.

And since we are all caught up in this language system, how we understand things is also determined by that system.

Ultimately, we are all trapped in language and we acquire our culture through language. We are speaking subjects.

To understand culture, you must understand the structures that function within it and the underlying patterns that shape it.

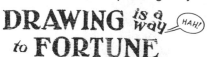

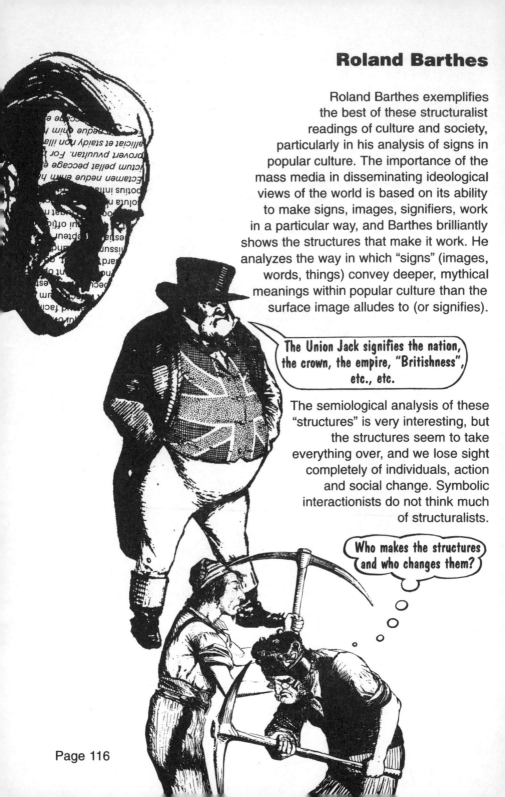

Roland Barthes

Roland Barthes exemplifies the best of these structuralist readings of culture and society, particularly in his analysis of signs in popular culture. The importance of the mass media in disseminating ideological views of the world is based on its ability to make signs, images, signifiers, work in a particular way, and Barthes brilliantly shows the structures that make it work. He analyzes the way in which "signs" (images, words, things) convey deeper, mythical meanings within popular culture than the surface image alludes to (or signifies).

> The Union Jack signifies the nation, the crown, the empire, "Britishness", etc., etc.

The semiological analysis of these "structures" is very interesting, but the structures seem to take everything over, and we lose sight completely of individuals, action and social change. Symbolic interactionists do not think much of structuralists.

> Who makes the structures and who changes them?

Multiple Sociologies

Structuralist approaches to culture and society bypassed mainstream sociology in that they tried to ignore each other. But, in effect, sociology has begun to unravel as a discipline as more and more areas of society or culture or the media become the site of specific study.

There are really many "sociologies" which reflect the extraordinary complexity of present-day society.

WOMEN'S STUDIES — BLACK STUDIES

MEDIA STUDIES

ASIAN STUDIES

CULTURAL STUDIES

All we can say is that the basic sociological problems – like is "social structure" more important than "individual agency"?, or does class still exist? – are still there, but they are approachable from a wide range of theoretical perspectives which seem to reflect what we call our "postmodern condition".

Postmodern means pick 'n' mix an' there ain't nothin' what is fix!

Feminism

The approach to traditional sociology that most critically undermines its claim to universal truth is that of feminism. From the welfare state to the media, feminists argue that sociology's explanations simply reproduce the idea that gender relations are "natural" and that women fulfil the social roles that are relevant and appropriate.

An awful lot of sociology simply didn't talk about women at all ...

We were invisible, except as the category of "mother".

The classic sociological debates about class are, quite simply, about men and class. If a man is a labourer, then that definition is treated as including the wife, which is not really very scientific.

In politics, discussions of the vote and of political rights were always, in effect, about the male, as discussions of citizenship showed.

The discourse of sociology has always been male, the gaze of sociologists has been male, and the obsession with work as not including domestic labour, is also male.

What is Feminism?

This is a question that preoccupies many people, including sociologists. We can define feminism as being a critique of society based on the inequalities that exist through gender roles and assumptions. Or, to put it another way, it is women demanding equality in terms of access to education, jobs, income, politics and power. It is a sociological fact that if you are a woman your chances of becoming prime minister, or a doctor, or a lawyer, are very much less than if you are a man.

The main feminist critique of sociology can be summed up as ...
1) Sociological research has always concentrated on men.
2) This research is then generalized to the whole population.
3) Areas of women's concerns, like reproduction, have been ignored.
4) Value-free research actually means sex-blind research, and women are presented in a distorted manner.
5) Sex and gender are not considered as important variables in analyzing the social, whereas they are critical.

Historically it has always been believed that women are not as good as men, although the extent of this belief has varied a lot. It is only in the last fifty years that women have actually achieved anything like equality, and it is still a limited achievement. Feminist critiques of society are based on the idea that people are actually born more or less equal and that it is only the way in which society organizes things that leads to discrimination.

Very recently in education it has become apparent that when girls are given the same opportunities as boys they actually do better in almost all subjects. This is rather worrying for boys because they have increasingly limited job opportunities in a world where technology is replacing muscle power as the dynamo of economic production.

In sociology, the debate about feminism gets very complicated because most sociologists were, and are, men. The way historical sociologists thought you should do sociological research was very much based on their outlook as men. For example, the whole debate about class – and in which class you were – was based on looking at what men did, and the women were seen as add-ons. It was as though women didn't exist except as mothers, wives and bolt-on bits of their husbands.

When sociology looked at politics and power, it looked at the public sphere, which is also predominantly male.

The private sphere, the domestic, was always ignored.

The division of labour between the public and the private was assumed to be "natural", that is, based in biology, and therefore not in need of investigation. When you consider that sociology was meant to be a "science of society" it seems odd that something so fundamental was taken for granted. That is not a very scientific attitude.

The programme that feminism
would advocate for a reconstructed
sociology would look something like this ...

1) Placing gender at the heart of all analysis, on a par
with class and race.

2) Criticizing all sociological theory for its "male" perspectives, which
means analyzing the unconscious, as well as conscious, attitudes
that structure sociologists' outlooks.

3) Analyzing the relationship between the public and
private spheres as being of central importance in
understanding how society functions.

4) Overhauling all of sociological theory.

One of the other outcomes of the
feminist critique of sociology was an
increasing awareness of the importance
of race, and anti-racism, which also
implied a fundamental criticism of the
categories of sociological theory.

Globalization

From the certainties of functionalism in the 1950s we have moved a long way to the present climate of sociological unease. Sociology's task has been completely redefined both by the undermining of traditional theoretical approaches and by the sudden and rapid transformation of post-war industrialized nation-states into what we can loosely call postmodern **global economies**.

Settled patterns of work, education, leisure and domestic life have all been transformed within the space of twenty years. A classic example is the coal-mining industry. Here you had what was termed "heavy" industry in which very traditional male patterns of work and leisure structured a class and domestic situation that was familiar and accepted.

In the space of 20 years the whole industry, particularly in places like South Wales, has disappeared, and with it has gone a whole way of life.

Now the women married to miners are the only ones working.

And they work in high-technology industries that themselves are coming to redefine the economy and society we operate in.

Some people now ask whether the old male working class still exists at all.

One of the fundamental problems affecting sociology is that in reality it has always assumed the **nation-state** as its sphere of analysis. American sociology focused on American society, economy, class structure and culture, and British sociology did the same for British society.

Some comparisons were made, but basically it was assumed that each nation-state had its own society and mores. Globalization breaks down the nation-state, removes the barriers between cultures, and does away with the limits imposed by concentrating on just one state.

Key Features of Globalization

1) The interconnectedness of all societies

2) Trans-national corporations that work in a global economy.

3) International economic integration, global production.

4) Trans-national media systems, the "global village".

5) Global consumerism and culture (Macdonaldization).

6) Global tourism, media imperialism.

The sociological question is whether this is a homogeneous one-way process or a contradictory and differential process. Once again, however, the whole process poses a large number of questions about how sociology relates to, and is limited by, the social conjunction within which it operates.

Michel Foucault

The long-standing criticism of sociology as being limited by the social and ideological ideas of its time was given greater emphasis by the work of **Michel Foucault** (1926–84). Foucault pointed out that sociology, like all other disciplines, was actually a set of ideas, an explanation of things, that was involved in the historical processes that it claimed to explain, and part of a power structure that reproduced those structures.

Sociology is not a value-free discipline, but a discourse about society that influences that society and its ideas about truth.

Foucault's concerns have centred around how knowledge is produced and utilized in a society, and how **power** and **discourse** are linked to knowledge. It is a sociology of knowledge in one sense, but it is also a radical deconstruction of the neat disciplinary boundaries that sociology has often attempted to construct.

Foucault's radicalism is part of what we call the postmodern turn in sociology – the refusal of all "meta-narratives" or grand theories about society and history. Foucault is anti-essentialist, anti-historical and very critical of attempts to argue that something like sociology is "value-free".

The emergence of sociology as a discipline is really bound up with particular descriptions of society, with a form of power in society, an apparatus — the educational and professional structures of sociology — and with the control of certain discourses about society.

Foucault's most radical work was concerned with sexuality and the body and the way these are constructed in discourse and social process. In his hands, sociology becomes an undermining of almost all empirical categories and a re-thinking of what it means to be human.

We've come a bit of a way from "social facts" and science, haven't we?

BLIMEY! IT'S THAT BIRD OFF THE COVER!

Jean Baudrillard

Baudrillard is another who drives a stake into the empirical heart of sociology. Baudrillard's view is that society doesn't exist. Or if it does, it is entirely composed of **signs**. This postmodern view sends some sociologists into a meta-theoretical frenzy, or a rage as it is empirically known. But all Baudrillard is really saying is that we live in a post-industrial, post-everything sort of society.

What I mean is that televisual communication, and its signs, have so come to dominate global reality that people have a great deal of difficulty deciding what is real.

Therefore, if everybody finds it difficult to understand the real, how can sociologists theoretically pin it down?

We live in a post-infotainment giant-screen Disney meta-world and sociology is about as useful as Egyptian trigonometry would be to an astronaut.

Yes, but what is sociology?

Research Methodology

Having discovered that sociological theories are as numerous as positions in the Kama Sutra, the question that may occur to the aspiring sociologist is, "How do you actually do sociology, rather than theorize it?" It should come as no surprise that the different theoretical approaches tend to favour different methodological approaches.

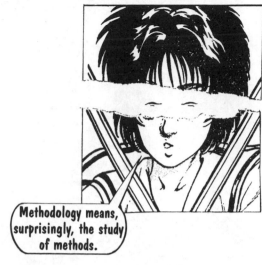

Methodology means, surprisingly, the study of methods.

I thought it was what Methodists do.

If you are going to study society, then you need first of all to think about how you observe and document it. Without empirical evidence – that is data, information, statistics, facts or whatever – you won't get very far. Although this has never stopped politicians.

What You Need To Be a Sociologist

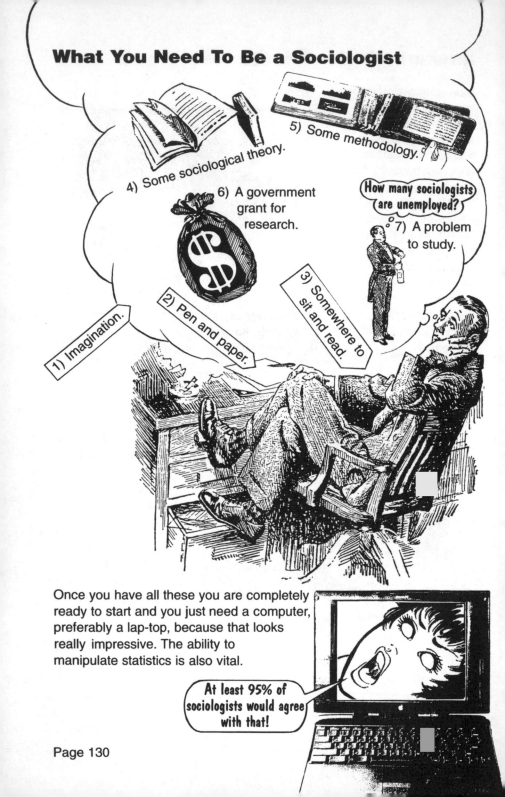

1) Imagination.

2) Pen and paper.

3) Somewhere to sit and read.

4) Some sociological theory.

5) Some methodology.

6) A government grant for research.

How many sociologists are unemployed?

7) A problem to study.

Once you have all these you are completely ready to start and you just need a computer, preferably a lap-top, because that looks really impressive. The ability to manipulate statistics is also vital.

At least 95% of sociologists would agree with that!

Sources

First of all there is the simple question of collecting information. Where do you get it from? Off the television or out of the papers is not a very good answer because these are secondary and unreliable sources. You have to work quite hard to find real information. It doesn't grow on the Internet.

Primary sources
This is the real McCoy, the information that you the sociologist produce through interview, research, observation, laboratory experiments or participant observation (or any other justifiable method you can think of). This is often of the social survey kind, and involves direct observation.

Is this primary, secondary or just bloody heavy?

Secondary sources
This is stuff that already exists, like government statistics, previous research, documentaries, autobiographies, newspaper reports, photographs, paintings, inquiry reports, Senate reports, things people tell you in the pub and anything you can find. The question of where information comes from is highly important here, since some sources are clearly more valid than others.

Questionnaires

Questionnaires are a common method of discovering sociological truths. You draw up a list of questions and then go and ask people. You write down what they say and then summarize it, coming to a general conclusion which you try to support with other evidence. It sounds simple but it can get a little complicated. You have to get the questions right.

The Hawthorne Effect

You have to make sure that questions are sensible, clear, not leading in one direction, unambiguous so that everyone understands them and answers the same question, and relevant to what you are trying to investigate. One of the major problems with all questionnaires (or surveys) is that people very much tend to say what they think the interviewer, or other people, expect them to say. Just as a police officer interviewing a suspect about a crime is not terribly likely to be told the truth.

The sociologist, like the police officer, has to apply a kind of rational procedure that can ferret out the truth by a combination of insight, thought and evidence.

A lot of a sociologist's time is spent trying to think up ways of producing hard information, and in then assessing what it means.

The effect of the interviewer or sociologist being in a particular situation and influencing it is known as the Hawthorne effect, after a phenomenon noted during the Hawthorne Studies into workplace behaviour in the US during the 1920s and 30s.

Interviews

The other way of trying to find out what people really think and do is through interviews. Short ones with lots of people, or very long ones with a few people. What is good about interviews? If they are well-structured then you can ask the same questions and get a balanced picture. You can produce quantifiable data.

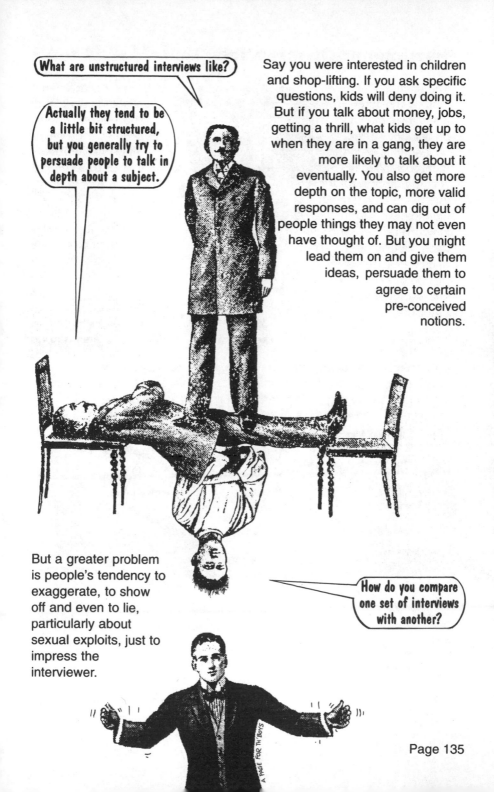

What are unstructured interviews like?

Actually they tend to be a little bit structured, but you generally try to persuade people to talk in depth about a subject.

Say you were interested in children and shop-lifting. If you ask specific questions, kids will deny doing it. But if you talk about money, jobs, getting a thrill, what kids get up to when they are in a gang, they are more likely to talk about it eventually. You also get more depth on the topic, more valid responses, and can dig out of people things they may not even have thought of. But you might lead them on and give them ideas, persuade them to agree to certain pre-conceived notions.

But a greater problem is people's tendency to exaggerate, to show off and even to lie, particularly about sexual exploits, just to impress the interviewer.

How do you compare one set of interviews with another?

Participant Observation

The ultimate form of long unstructured interviews is participant observation, which means going to live with the group you are interested in. A famous example was **John Howard Griffin**, who dyed his skin black and lived as a black man in the southern states of America (1960).

Boy, did I learn some things!

Another famous instance was **Hunter Thompson**, who lived with a bunch of Hell's Angels and observed their culture (1967).

I nearly got killed for my efforts!

Participant observation came from social anthropology, where practitioners went and lived amongst the "primitive" cultures they were studying. Anthropologists look at the culture as a whole, whereas sociologists tend to study small groups within complex cultures.

One of the really basic problems with it is that it takes forever.

And you tend to start liking the people you are with. You don't remain sufficiently distanced.

The Statistical Approach

At the other end of the research spectrum, some sociologists go for the systematic scientific approach using number-crunching, sampling, variable controls and the quantification of results. The advent of massive computer power and of the general availability of statistics means that this kind of analytic approach is far easier now than it was just 20 years ago. In theory, we therefore have far more reliable information about society as a whole, the levels of unemployment, divorce, the numbers of people in education and so on.

Constructing social samples and analyzing the information you receive in statistical terms is now quite a large part of sociological study.

But do we know more about society as a result of all this statistical evidence?

Only if we know where the statistics came from, how they were collected and how they were analyzed.

The problem with all of these approaches is that at the end of the day they are all based on what **theoretical position** you adopt to explain and understand the society you see in front of you.

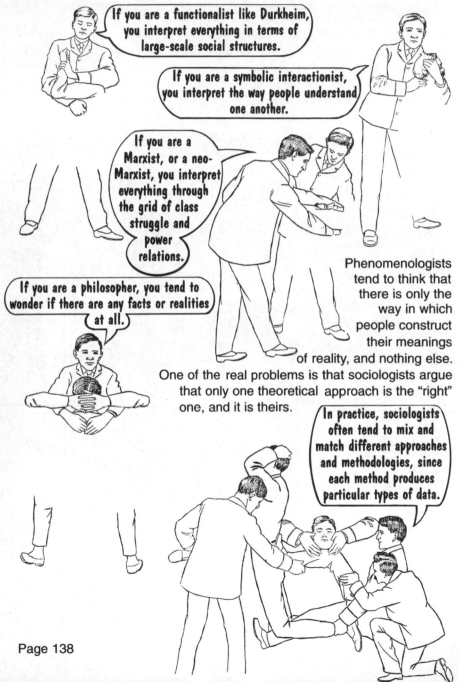

If you are a functionalist like Durkheim, you interpret everything in terms of large-scale social structures.

If you are a symbolic interactionist, you interpret the way people understand one another.

If you are a Marxist, or a neo-Marxist, you interpret everything through the grid of class struggle and power relations.

If you are a philosopher, you tend to wonder if there are any facts or realities at all.

Phenomenologists tend to think that there is only the way in which people construct their meanings of reality, and nothing else. One of the real problems is that sociologists argue that only one theoretical approach is the "right" one, and it is theirs.

In practice, sociologists often tend to mix and match different approaches and methodologies, since each method produces particular types of data.

What is CULTURE?

After adopting a particular theoretical approach, and then possibly a methodology that complements it, the sociologist then has to confront a number of problems that make up the key areas of debate in modern sociology. The most difficult problem is what sociologists call CULTURE, one of those words that creates endless debates. Here are some working definitions of what the word might mean.

1) The norms, values, ideas and ways of doing things in a particular society. This is the broad definition.

2) All of the means of communication, art, material things and objects that a society has in common. The cultivation of the mind, the civilization and learning of a society. This is the narrower definition.

3) The ways of life shared by a particular group (e.g. working-class culture).

4) The practices that produce meaning in a society (signifying practices).

The original use of the term "culture" came from farming, and meant the cultivation or development of the land. This grew into a notion of civilized, as opposed to natural, behaviour, and came to mean the way in which upper-class groups behaved. A later Enlightenment notion was that all society was developing towards a higher, more complex culture based on science and rationality. It was at this point that the *nature/culture* divide began, and led to the idea of the dominance of industrial culture over backward nature.

During the 19th century the idea of "high culture", as the best of art and thought and music, took over and sociologists' approach to the idea of culture became more confused. In the 20th century, popular culture arrived on the scene and made the whole debate even more tortured. Television culture reduced sociologists simply to analyzing the way in which culture in general operated as a "signifying system".

The Problem of Culture

The problem with understanding the "culture" of a society is that the most general idea of culture – an *entire* way of life – virtually covers the whole of sociology. The reason people tend to behave in a particular way, say at weddings, family gatherings or other social events, is that this kind of behaviour is determined by the culture that people live in. So sociologists have to try refining the idea of culture all the time and even explaining what the different "cultures" are. We can talk about "popular culture", "mass culture", "high culture" and people who are "uncultured".

Culture in the broadest sense is all of the modes of thought, behaviour, interaction and communication handed down from generation to generation via language, and all other modes of communicating, including gesture, painting, writing, architecture, music, fashion, food and so on. Culture is really the way that a large group of people do things, built up over time and transmitted from one generation to the next. Without culture we would be like animals. In fact, in times of war, when the culture breaks down, that is what humans seem to regress to. Our culture is a way of behaving that helps people make sense of the world and makes sure everybody knows what they are supposed to be doing.

Culture and Language

Culture really is a tricky thing to pin down, so some sociologists ignore it completely and concentrate on statistics. It is such an all-encompassing concept that perhaps it is easier to break it down into bits. What are the *elements* of culture? Language, ideas, norms and values, and material culture – and the way they all interrelate. Language is the key that distinguishes man from animals and is the mode in which all culture is communicated and transmitted.

Some even think that language determines culture, so that, for example, being Chinese is very bound up with the language itself (this is known as the linguistic-relativity hypothesis).

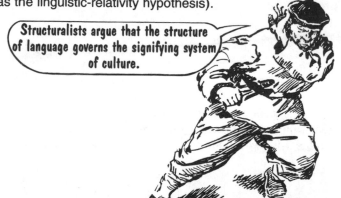

Social Norms

Culture operates through agreed sets of rules called social norms (or codes or mores). In settled cultures, the social norms are clear and distinct. In the Christian British society of the 19th century, for example, there was a high degree of social conformity and acceptance of Christian family values as being the basis on which social norms operated.

We could call this British Imperial culture, and if you were white and middle-class it seemed like a very good thing.

Everybody knew their place, social etiquette was clear, and the lower orders were very respectful.

In the 20th century, there were massive changes to the way culture was shaped and experienced. This is often understood as being the rise of "mass culture", which means that rather than aristocratic and Christian values, the values of entertainment, pleasure and secularism took hold.

Mass Culture

"Mass culture", it was claimed, was the product of the industrialization and commercialization of culture, which meant that newspapers, films and other cultural products were now produced in a more organized and efficient way with the deliberate aim of making money out of their consumption. Sociologists of the Frankfurt school put forward the argument that this new mass culture was being imposed from above by a new commercial bourgeoisie who recognized the possibilities in a new wage-earning proletariat with disposable income and a desire to be distracted from everyday life. This pessimistic sociological outlook about culture is not shared by everyone.

Murder Stalks The Carnival

There are those who argue that this is not mass culture but "popular culture", and that it is critical of traditional "high culture" and is therefore a good thing.

Girl on the RUN

Hollywood movies are anti-establishment, critical and celebratory of everyday life.

What, you mean like *Gone With the Wind* or *The Sound of Music?*

Class and Stratification

One theme that runs throughout popular or mass culture is the existence of the rich and the poor. Social stratification seems to exist in all societies, even the supposedly equal Communist societies. So how does one explain this? Stratification means that different groups in society occupy different places within the pecking order. There are rich and poor, and people who live down subways. There are Royal Families and there are homeless people. There are farmers and factory workers. Sociologists have long noted that the members of a particular group seem to have common outlooks, similar interests and distinct life styles. People's experience of life tends to be much the same as the rest of their group.

This is what leads sociologists to think that groups are more important in society than individuals.

The functionalists and the social system side argue that stratification is necessary, and the conflict theorists argue that it is the result of an unequal distribution of power and wealth.

Marx argued very clearly that class was the fundamental stratification in society, and that was all there was to say about it.

Explaining Social Inequality

Marx introduced into sociology the important idea of class, and an explanation of where social inequality came from. He didn't say that some people were poor because they were immoral and hence deserved to be, but argued that control of economic resources and wealth defined a class structure. The position you were born into in this class structure then determined the likely outcome of your health, wealth, education and future occupation. This leads to a number of questions.

Marxists argue that class is determined by the relationship to the means of production, and that consciousness and culture follow from that. Weberians say that class reflects an individual's position in the market place. What Weber said was,

Yes, there *are* classes in society, but inequality can't be explained just in terms of ownership and property.

Marx argued that,

In essence, economic relations determine *everything* else — the cultural, the personal, the law, the entire "superstructure" of what I call **ideology**.

There are more things to class than just economics, although that is still important.

There are classes, but there is also the problem of status and of parties, and of religion and culture.

The culture of a society is the culture of the ruling class.

Marx's model cannot explain the middle classes who constitute an ever-growing and powerful group.

Does Class Matter?

Everyone in sociology says that Weber's work is a debate with the ghost of Marx, and the argument over class rumbles on.

Listen, my spectral friend, you wrote when industrial society was still being formed. So it was difficult to predict what would happen. Society is much more complex than you imagined.

Humbug! The spectre of Communism will wander around until the end of time.

However, understanding how complex class society has become needs a 20th century viewpoint. Class, status, hierarchy and social position are as much to do with cultural ideas as with straight economic power.

At the end of the day, it is about economic power. However you dress it up, that is what determines people's life chances. "Behind every great fortune there is a great crime."

A pair of sociologists known as Davis and Moore (1945) argued that stratification existed in all known societies, and breezily decided it was therefore a functional necessity of society. As such, it usefully ensured that the best people got the top jobs. Clearly this is an exaggeration. Members of the upper classes and élites regularly get access to education and jobs that are denied to other people.

This brings us to the question of **social mobility** and **meritocracy**.

Is an élite maintained in society because members of that élite have greater access to wealth, education, power, contacts and rewards or because they are naturally better at things?

With aristocrats in prison for fraud and drugs, with members of the Royal Family behaving like teenagers in a soap opera, one could be forgiven for thinking that being upper-class is coterminous with in-bred stupidity.

So, do we have a classless society in which everyone has equal life opportunities? Many sociologists have argued that we are moving towards a classless society, and that class has virtually disappeared as a significant sociological fact.

So why do so many people in Britain identify themselves by class?

Is class defined by wealth, by education, or by hereditary principles?

Why do children from the manual working classes, as we used to call them, do so badly in education and jobs?

Why are the sons and daughters of the professional middle classes over-represented in universities?

Why do people find it so necessary always to say that class has "disappeared"?

The Underclass

Just when it felt safe to be "de-classed", sociologists decided that the new problem was the **underclass**. This new group of people are those who, through lack of employment, skills, wealth or property, appear to be virtually outside ordinary society. The underclass really means people who are superfluous in a globalized economy where production can be moved around the world to the cheapest place.

So the unskilled in the advanced capitalist countries are replaced by cheap labour in the developing world, or by technology.

The unemployed are always blamed for being unemployed, and then social scientists like Charles Murray come along with their theories of the underclass and say that it exists because the state gives them "too much money".

Are you serious — the state gives us too much money?

Charles Murray reckons that if you give people welfare benefits, they become "dependent" on them and then they don't want to work, and hey presto, you have an underclass. All you need to do is take the money away and then they'll become socially responsible and get jobs.

Welfare and Poverty

The problem of the underclass raises the whole question of wealth, poverty and the 20th century phenomenon of the welfare state. Questions like "Why are people poor?" lead to interesting sociological debates about what the function of welfare is.

Sir William Beveridge (1879–1963), director of the London School of Economics, invented the welfare state after the Second World War, with the aim that it would provide for those who, through no fault of their own, were unemployed, ill, old or simply poor. This social democratic idea sounds very reasonable, but many Conservatives opposed it then, and even more oppose it now.

Sociology today is very much bound up with the arguments about the welfare state.

Market liberals strongly argue that the welfare state interferes with individual freedoms.

At one level it is a debate about how society should work. Should it be rampantly capitalist or does the community come first?

Beveridge's welfare state was based on essentially social-democratic ideas in which the concept of "citizenship" is key. The modern idea of the nation-state is really one of a community of citizens who all have common rights and freedoms. This idea of rights and freedoms constantly comes up against the realities of economic power, ownership and educational and political power.

My ideas about the post-war welfare state were meant to cement the relationship between "citizenship" and "welfare", and to enshrine the rights of individuals to health, employment, education and housing.

From its very inception, we Conservatives have attacked the idea of the welfare state as being an infringement on the free play of market forces, which we claim really dictate how societies function.

NAY!

These battles within sociology – and social policy – have become very marked in the last decade, with free-marketeers in power in Britain and America attempting to enforce their ideas on welfare, employment, education, health and the economy. These political battles demonstrate how closely social theory is linked to historical change and development, and how much the political climate influences how sociology operates.

Free-marketeers regularly attack the whole idea of sociology, claiming that society is not an observable entity.

Either it's an illusion or it's simply the market forces that connect people.

What About the Family?

Strangely enough, the free-marketeers also claim that the family is a vital unit in society, and often claim that it is disintegrating and has to be supported. A strange view, since their ideology usually claims "let the market decide".

From functionalists to postmodernists, everyone has some kind of argument about what role the family plays in society, and why. The absolutely central question is whether or not the family is a universal institution in all societies, and to what extent does it vary?

As this is a family book we'll have a polite quiz on these questions to keep everyone amused. The trick is to spot the different theoretical approaches to...

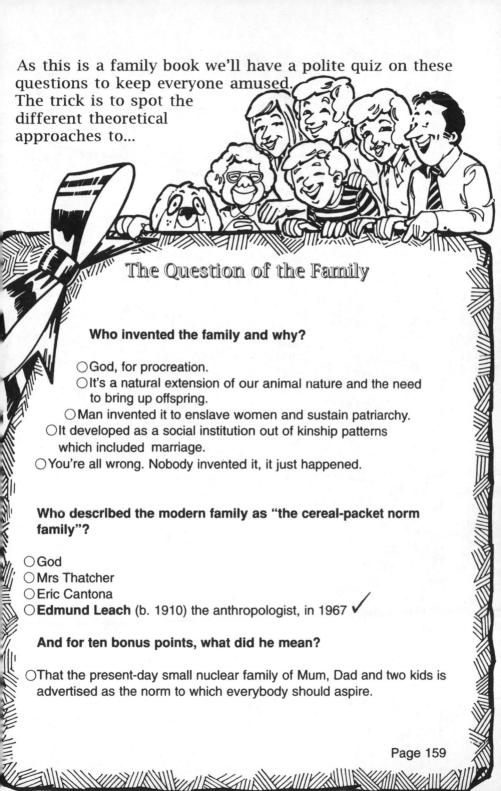

The Question of the Family

Who invented the family and why?

○ God, for procreation.
○ It's a natural extension of our animal nature and the need to bring up offspring.
○ Man invented it to enslave women and sustain patriarchy.
○ It developed as a social institution out of kinship patterns which included marriage.
○ You're all wrong. Nobody invented it, it just happened.

Who described the modern family as "the cereal-packet norm family"?

○ God
○ Mrs Thatcher
○ Eric Cantona
○ **Edmund Leach** (b. 1910) the anthropologist, in 1967 ✓

And for ten bonus points, what did he mean?

○ That the present-day small nuclear family of Mum, Dad and two kids is advertised as the norm to which everybody should aspire.

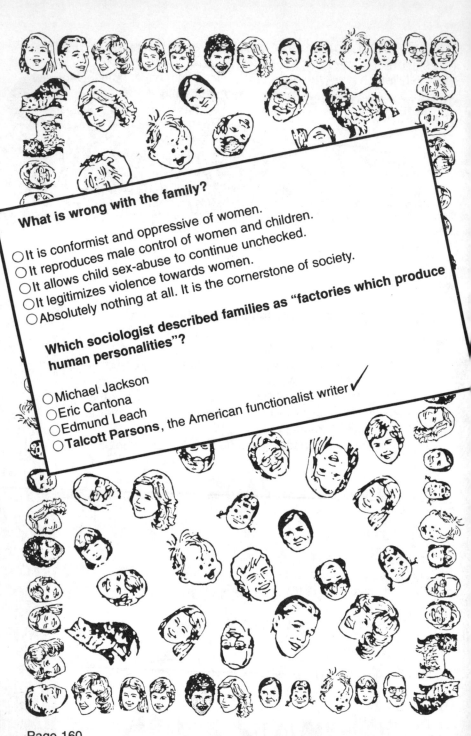

What is wrong with the family?

○ It is conformist and oppressive of women.
○ It reproduces male control of women and children.
○ It allows child sex-abuse to continue unchecked.
○ It legitimizes violence towards women.
○ Absolutely nothing at all. It is the cornerstone of society.

Which sociologist described families as "factories which produce human personalities"?

○ Michael Jackson
○ Eric Cantona
○ Edmund Leach
○ **Talcott Parsons**, the American functionalist writer ✓

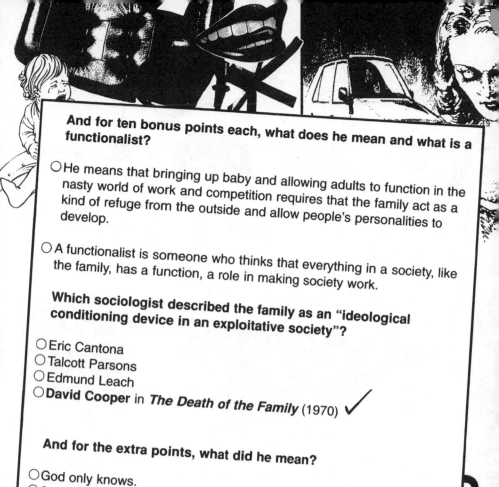

And for ten bonus points each, what does he mean and what is a functionalist?

○ He means that bringing up baby and allowing adults to function in the nasty world of work and competition requires that the family act as a kind of refuge from the outside and allow people's personalities to develop.

○ A functionalist is someone who thinks that everything in a society, like the family, has a function, a role in making society work.

Which sociologist described the family as an "ideological conditioning device in an exploitative society"?

○ Eric Cantona
○ Talcott Parsons
○ Edmund Leach
○ **David Cooper** in *The Death of the Family* (1970) ✓

And for the extra points, what did he mean?

○ God only knows.
○ Something not very nice.
○ That the family is the place where children are socialized into conforming to society's rules which are made up by the people who run things.
○ Is he a functionalist?

How do you define the family?

○ Mum, Dad and two kids who watch television together.
○ An outmoded form of social oppression that leads to the exploitation of women and the abuse of children.
○ The loving heart of God's faith and the true sanctity of marriage.
○ A nice idea if you can make it work. Even the Royal Family can't make it work.

Whose fault is that?

○ The family is so important in sociology simply because that is where society is reproduced in its most basic form, the individual. Wherever you start in sociology you have to have some idea of how to conceptualize the family, how it changes and what the connection between the family and society is.

As we said earlier, the forms of socialization that exist in society are a very important part of shaping the development of individuals. Each part of the socialization process receives different emphasis by different kinds of sociologists.

For a long time, however, education has received sociological attention as being the central force that reproduces the culture and ideas of a society. Trainee sociologists will by now realize that the different schools of thought have varying explanations of how education functions, and what it is for.

The Sociology of Education

Mass education is a very new thing historically, and has only been widespread since the Second World War. Before that, serious education was the preserve of the wealthy and the middle classes. Working-class students tended not to do as well in education as their middle-class colleagues.

In a famous book that crytallizes these debates, *Learning to Labour: How Working-Class Kids Get Working-Class Jobs* (1977), Paul Willis looked at the way in which working-class boys rejected the middle-class values of school and thus condemned themselves to working-class jobs.

Althusser

The French Marxist **Louis Althusser** (1918–90) argued, rather like Gramsci, that education played an important role in spreading bourgeois ideology or reproducing the dominant culture. Most sociologists agree that education does reproduce the culture, but they differ about whether or not this is an innocent process.

Althusser is quite certain that it is profoundly ideological.

The sociology of education then demands analysis of the structures of education, what is taught, who teaches it to whom, and what outcomes this has for the functioning of society.

Class, language, gender, race and intelligence all become key issues in trying to link educational processes to the way people end up perceiving themselves, and therefore acting in society.

Althusser also thought that the mass media were an important means of ideological control in modern society (as do many Marxists and cultural critics) and one of the primary definers of our culture today. There are many sociologists who in fact argue that the mass media, particularly television, influence the process of socialization as much as the family or school. If this is true, it begs a lot of questions about how we do sociology today.

Traditional sociology has not really taken that much notice of the mass media, despite the fact that television has clearly changed the whole culture of industrialized countries.

Television has utterly changed the way politics is conducted, and has changed our leisure culture from being a public, communal culture into a home-based private culture.

If Abraham Lincoln were alive today he would never be elected. He's far too ugly to appear on television.

Postmodern Hyperreality

We mentioned Jean Baudrillard earlier, who argued that we live in such a media-saturated society that it is now "hyperreal". There is no reality, just simulations that people take for real. This is a million miles, sociologically speaking, from empirical analysis, social facts and class analysis. If Baudrillard is right, then most sociology can pack up and go to a rest home.

The only analysis we need now is of images and ideology.

Baudrillard does, however, suggest that in some ways people have greater freedom in this postmodern world to pick whatever images and lifestyles they like, which can sound positive.

The jury is still out on the postmodern debate, and some people argue that it is itself just a simulation of a theory.

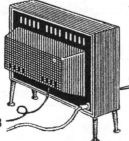

Television is about as real as watching a goldfish bowl and thinking that's what the sea is like.

Television and Crime

One area where television, sociology and society meet head-on is in the representations of crime and deviance. Old-fashioned sociology used to talk about the "criminal mind", the "criminal personality" or even the "criminal classes". Now television sets the agenda for how people perceive crime and criminality.

In another important book, *Policing the Crisis* (1978), a group of sociologists examined the way in which the media began to report and exaggerate crime, in particular, mugging. They then examined how this sort of "moral panic" spread throughout society and transformed everyone's ideas about crime. The media have since taken up crime as an exciting, sexy and threatening topic to fill up the schedules.

Sociology and Criminology

Sociology has a long history of discussing crime in society, from Durkheim on suicide to classic studies of gangs in Chicago. Debates about the causes of crime and deviance are very important, but if the media now totally control social ideas about crime, then we are in a wholly different paradigm. *Policing the Crisis* examined the ways in which the media portrayed certain crimes, like mugging, as "black" crimes.

The importance of this analysis was that it looked at the creation of stereotypes in the media that relied on unconscious associations rather than overt facts.

The power of these images to shape ideas about crime, race and society does suggest that we now live in a different kind of society in which the media, in little understood ways, constantly reshapes culture.

Youth culture is particularly dominated by popular media images, and this impacts on education, fashion, identity and individual self-image.

The certainties with which sociology started in the 19th century, the idea of a positive, rational science and of objectivity and neutrality, now look like many other 19th century views – cumbersome, grandiose and slightly ridiculous. Above all else, it is clear that sociology is a product of its time and reflects the ideas and interests of the social groups who control it. What began as critical social theory, as almost a philosophical enterprise to understand society and man, has ended as a profession which tries to justify its status and objectives by elaborating all the paraphernalia of a science – or what Michel Foucault calls a discourse – in order to shore up the creaking 19th century edifice.

The rise of a critical feminism, and an understanding of the ethnocentrism at the heart of sociology, the critique of imperialism which links the Western world's development to the under-development of the Third World, all undermine the assumptions that sociology makes about **how** to study society.

The Death of Sociology?

Is sociology dead? As a grand theory, or set of theories that explain everything in a particular society, probably yes. As an impulse to develop a critical understanding of what makes human society possible, of how being human is constantly being redefined, probably no.

Present-day society is bewildering in its speed of transformation, new technology, globalization, incredible wealth and mass unemployment linked by a global media and postmodern wars. These problems give sociologists nightmares. Before they have completed their ten-year research programme, the world has moved on and the social structure they were considering has transmuted into something else.

Sociology has therefore to become a critical, political activity as well as an academic activity.

It also has to recognize that almost every area of society it considers is now represented, transformed and shaped by a global culture that pays little attention to old boundaries.

We are probably all going to be urban creatures by the middle of the next century, and that is a strange reality.

Sociology is a generic name for all of the approaches to understanding human behaviour in its modern inter-social forms.

THANKS TO LITZA JANSZ FOR PERMISSION TO USE HER AMAZONIAN ANDROID CHARACTER

The end? Well, nearly. Of course, this is only one book about sociology and only one view. Turn the page for plenty of others... →→→→→

Further Reading

There are many introductions to sociology, from two-page revision sheets to huge American tomes that attempt to cover everything, and the English versions are moving that way. Sociology is such a vast subject that it is almost impossible for any small introduction to cover everything, or even to sketch in the main problems. Most academic introductions try to cover the basics, with varying degrees of success. There is not a lot of difference between many of these academic introductions, although some of the newer ones are more user-friendly. There is no substitute for reading the original texts, but they can be intimidating and the reader needs a way in.

Recommended introductory reading:
Abbot, P. & Wallace, C., **An Introduction to Sociology: Feminist Perspectives**. Routledge, London 1990
Berger, P., **Invitation to Sociology**. Penguin, London 1966
Calvert, P. & Calvert, S., **Sociology Today**. Harvester Wheatsheaf, Hemel Hempstead 1992
Craib, I., **Modern Social Theory**. Heinemann, London 1968
Giddens, A., **Sociology**. Macmillan, Basingstoke 1982
Marsh, I. et al, **Sociology in Focus**. Causeway Press, Ormskirk 1996
Marshall, G., **In Praise of Sociology**. Unwin Hyman, London 1990
Mills, C.W., **The Sociological Imagination**. Oxford University Press, New York 1959
Moore, S., **Sociology Alive**. Stanley Thornes, Cheltenham 1987
Nisbet, R., **The Sociological Tradition**. Heinemann, London 1967
O'Donnell, M., **A New Introduction to Sociology**. Thomas Nelson, London 1992
Scott, J., **Sociological Theory**. Edward Elgar, Cheltenham 1995
Slattery, M., **Key Ideas in Sociology**. Sage Publications, London 1993
Swingewood, A., **A Short History of Sociological Thought**. Macmillan, London 1984

More advanced reading:
Bell, C. & Roberts, H., **Social Researching**. Routledge, London 1984
Bourdieu, P., **Sociology in Question**. Sage Publications, London 1993
Crowley, H. & Himmelweit, S., **Knowing Women**. Polity Press, Cambridge 1992
Durkheim, E., **The Rules of Sociological Method**. The Free Press, New York 1938

Fletcher, R., **The Making of Sociology**. Nelson University Paperbacks, London 1972

Giddens, A., **The Consequences of Modernity**. Polity Press, Cambridge 1990

Hall, S. & Held, D., **Modernity and its Futures**. Polity Press, Cambridge 1992

Jones, P., **Studying Society: Sociological Theories and Research Practices**. Collins Harvill, London 1993

Lee, D. & Newby, H., **The Problem of Sociology**. Hutchinson, London 1983

Maynard, M., **Sociological Theory**. Longman, London 1989

McQuail, D., **Mass Communication Theory**. Sage Publications, London 1983

Merton, R. et al, **Sociology Today**. Basic Books, New York 1959

Morrison, R., **Marx, Durkheim, Weber**. Sage Publications, London 1995

Mouzolis, N., **Sociological Theory: What Went Wrong?** Routledge, London 1995

Pareto, V., **A Treatise on General Sociology**. Dover Publications, New York 1963

Parsons, T., **Essays in Sociological Theory**. The Free Press, Glencoe, Illinois 1964

Sherman, H. & Wood, J., **Sociology**. Harper & Row, New York 1979

Wallace, R., **Feminism and Sociological Theory**. Sage Publications, Newbury Park, California 1989

Waters, M., **Modern Sociological Theory**. Sage Publications, London 1994

Weber, M., **The Protestant Ethic and the Spirit of Capitalism**. Simon & Schuster, New York 1980

Whelehan, I., **Modern Feminist Thought**. Edinburgh University Press, 1995

Worsley, P. (ed.), **Modern Sociology: Introductory Readings**. Penguin, London 1970

Typesetting by Goodfellow & Egan, Cambridge